The ULTIMATE GUIDE to an AFFORDABLE Disney World VACATION

WITHDRAWN

HOW TO EASILY SAVE THOUSANDS ON YOUR NEXT TRIP!

KEVIN BARRY

The Ultimate Guide to an Affordable Disney World Vacation
by Kevin Barry

Edited by Emily Juhnke
Photography by Mike Billick

http://www.FrugalMouse.com

© **2016 Frugal Enterprises, LLC**
ISBN 978-0-9974363-1-0

All rights reserved. No portion of this book may be reproduced in any form without permission from the publisher, except as permitted by U.S. copyright law.

For permissions contact: kevin@FrugalMouse.com

This book is unauthorized and unofficial. It has not been reviewed by The Walt Disney Company and is in no way authorized, endorsed or approved by the company, it's sponsors, partners or affiliates.

CONTENTS

Boyle County Public Library

OTHER DISCOUNTS AND
MONEY-SAVING TIPS 101

HOW MUCH DID WE SAVE? 115

Claim Your FREE
Bonus Chapter!

Would you like to learn even more about how to make the most of your Disney vacation? As a token of my thanks to you for purchasing and reading this book, I've written an additional bonus chapter that is FREE and available only to you - the readers.

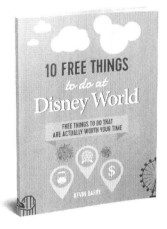

This chapter is titled *My Favorite Free Things To Do at Disney World*. I'll re-view free things to do at the parks and resorts that are actually worth your time.

I've personally done each of the things I outline in the chapter, and I can vouch that they are not just time wasters. They are well worth taking the time to do. I hope they help you get even more enjoyment out of your next trip down to Disney!

To claim your free copy of the bonus chapter, simply go to
http://www.FrugalMouse.com/bonus
You're welcome to share this link with your friends and family as well!

INTRODUCTION

Take a moment to imagine yourself planning a family trip to Disney World without having an overwhelming amount of stress about how you're going to afford it. Can you picture it?

We all know that there can be many costs associated with such a big trip. It might be difficult to imagine keeping everyone happy, making the trip affordable and enjoying the experience all at the same time. My name is Kevin, and I'm here to help you make the financial side of your next family vacation to Disney as worry free as possible.

Today, Disney World is more popular than ever: Tens of millions of people take a trip to central Florida every year to visit "the happiest place on earth." However, the huge costs involved with a Disney vacation is still a problem that many families face. Some might have to plan ahead and save for years in advance of making the trip.

I grew up in Philadelphia. When I was young, my family would go to Disney once every four years. When you're a kid, that can feel like an eternity between trips. It simply was too expensive for us to be able to go more frequently than that. I know this is the reality for many people today.

As I got older, and being the huge Disney fan that I am, I began looking into ways to help keep the cost of Disney vacations down. About five years ago, I started a website called Frugal Mouse (www.frugalmouse.com) as a way to share all of the money-saving strategies and tips I came across. The site still serves that same purpose today. The book you are reading now was born out of the spirit of Frugal Mouse and out of my desire to go to Disney World more often.

All that you will read in this book has been tried and tested by myself, as well as by my friends and family. Using these strategies, I've been able to go to Disney World at least once a year for the past 10 years. This, of course, was dependent on the vacation time I had available. I was also able to cut my costs down from thousands to just hundreds of dollars for two people.

Even though the tips in this book are geared toward Disney World, they can also be applied to any type of travel! Chapter 1: Travel To Disney, for example, includes tips for purchasing flights and rental cars that can easily be used regardless of where you're traveling to.

Over the course of this book, we'll follow the Barry family: a hypothetical family of four in the process of planning their next trip to Disney World. We have Mom Barry; Dad Barry; Bobby, a young teenager; and Susy, an older child. The high cost of trips to Florida have only allowed them to vacation there every few years. It is their dream to be able to increase that to once every other year, but that will only be possible if they find ways to greatly reduce their vacation expenses. Within this book, they'll learn how to do that and turn their dream into a reality!

The costs of their previous Disney vacation can be broken down into the following:

- **Flights:** $1,000   ($250/person)
- **Resort:** $900   ($180/night)
- **Park Tickets:** $1,580   (4-day park hopper)
- **Food:** $700
- **Total:**   **$4,180**

That is quite a lot of money for the Barry family, which is why they need to find ways to cut those costs.

WHAT THIS BOOK IS AND IS NOT

I've read many websites and books that provide suggestions of ways to save money at Disney. My issue with many of those money-saving "tips" has been that they seem to forget that, when you're at Disney World, you're also on vacation. If I were to follow their suggestions, I wouldn't have near as much fun at Disney. I don't think you and your family would either.

I'm not going to suggest that you eat every single meal in your hotel room. I'm not going to encourage you to go to the fixins' bar in Cosmic Ray's Starlight Cafe and make a lettuce, tomato and ketchup sandwich for lunch. I would never buy a double cheeseburger and then ask for a second bun so that I could make another burger out of it.

I'm also not going to spend a lot of time focusing on the small ticket items that would probably only save you a dollar or two here and there. I'm going to help you save on your big ticket items such as flights, park admission tickets, hotels and food. As mentioned, everything that you will read in this book I have personally used and will continue to use on my future trips.

Remember: When you're at Disney World, you're on a vacation. The purpose of vacations is to relax, get away, spend time with family and friends, and make memories that will last you a lifetime. If you're continuously worrying about the major costs of your trip, you won't have as much time to focus on those things. That's what this book is going to help you with. After you've finished reading it, my hope is that you are inspired and excited about the idea of planning your next family vacation to Disney!

GETTING TO DISNEY

Getting there is half the fun, right?

In this first chapter, our main focus is going to be on how to get to Orlando via airplane. I'll also throw in a few tips for car travel, in case you happen to be within driving distance. In addition, there will be a section with tips on renting a car for your time at Disney.

Everyone has their own level of tolerance when it comes to long road trips. For me, it's about eight hours. If I can't get somewhere in a car in eight hours or less, I'll look into flight options to get me there much faster.

My family did drive to Disney once, and it was the first and last time we attempted that. An 18-hour drive from Philadelphia to Orlando in the old Ford station wagon did not add up to a very enjoyable trip. We did set up a TV and our Nintendo in the back seat, which made it less painful for my brother and me. However, we also weren't the ones stuck driving.

When it comes to flying vs. driving, you'll have to run some numbers to see what makes the most sense in your situation. Many people opt to drive long distances because of the high price of flights. If this is true for you,

you definitely want to continue reading because I will help you find ways to save money on those flights.

Let's take a look at our family, the Barrys, to see how much their flight from Philadelphia to Orlando will cost them. The only feasible time for them to go to Disney is when the kids are out of school, so that means making the trip sometime in May, June, July or August. Unfortunately for them, those are also some of the peak months for air travel. This means potentially expensive flights. They've decided that they want to make their trip in May right after the kids are out of school so that they can get their summer off to a great and exciting start.

A search of airfares from Philadelphia to Orlando puts prices in the $200 - $300 range per round-trip ticket. For simplicity's sake, we'll say that, on average, flights will be $250/person. For a family of four, that will put flight prices at $1,000 total. This is a huge portion of the Barry's total vacation budget.

Here's the deal: The Barry family can't afford to spend $1,000 on flights to get them to Orlando. Let's dive into some options to get them to Disney World for much, much cheaper than that. We'll also discuss ways to apply these strategies to your own Disney vacation!

What You Will Learn in this Chapter:
- When the best time is to book your flights
- How to search for the cheapest flights
- How to use frequent flyer miles for free flights
- What a hidden city fare is
- How to use Priceline.com to bid on cheap rental cars
- Tips to save money when driving to Disney

WHEN IS THE BEST TIME TO BOOK FLIGHTS?

The question of when to book flights comes across my email almost on a daily basis. It is true that, when you purchase flights, there are several factors that can have a huge impact on the price that you pay. The person sitting next to you on your flight could **have paid $100 more or $100 less than you,** depending on many variables.

Airline fares are fluid. They are constantly being updated based on the number of searches for a particular flight, how full that flight is, how far in advance you are looking and many other factors.

You know you're in Orlando when it's time to get on the airport tram!

Generally, airline fares are based on supply and demand. Airlines might charge more for flights on very popular or limited routes, simply because they can. Sometimes a short, hour-long flight could cost $600+, but a cross-country flight might only be $300. The cross-country flight probably costs the airline much more to operate, but they can charge much more for the shorter flights if there is a higher demand for those.

THE WORST (AND MOST EXPENSIVE) TIMES TO FLY

It might seem that the prices for airline tickets are constantly changing without any pattern or logical reason. However, there are a few times when it is best to avoid flying if you can. Flights at certain times of the year, along with when you actually buy the tickets, can really drive the cost up. Avoiding them can help you save hundreds of dollars on a plane ticket. We'll discuss some particular examples below.

Last-Minute Flights

The closer it gets to the departure date for a flight, the higher the prices will become. This is due to several reasons, including the following:

- Planes fill up as the departure date nears, so the old supply/demand pricing takes effect and drives prices up.

- When people are booking last-minute flights, they won't have much flexibility. Airlines know this, hence the higher prices.

Data from a Cheapair.com study backs that up. According to the study, the absolute worst time to book a flight is one day out, followed by two days out, followed by three days out, and so on up to about 13 days out.

To avoid paying unnecessarily high prices for your tickets, you should book them at least two weeks in advance.

Fridays - Sundays

We all love the idea of taking off for the weekend on an exciting, two-day getaway. Due to the high number of weekend flyers, rates are generally higher Fridays through Sundays than they are during the middle of the week. In addition, many business flyers travel home on Fridays and back out again on Sundays, which increases both the demand and prices of tickets on those days. Avoid traveling on the weekends, if you can.

Holidays

Thanksgiving and Christmas, respectively, are the two busiest times of the year for travel. These, along with other holidays, are exceptionally expensive times to fly because of the increase in demand for tickets.

A 2014 study by SkyScanner revealed that the cheapest time to book Christmas flights is the first week of October, and the best time to book for Thanksgiving is the end of September. Just to reiterate, while these tend to be the cheapest times to book, you still will pay a premium to fly around the holidays. If you are planning to head down to Disney for the holidays, be sure to book early!

Summer Travel

In addition to weekends and holidays, summer is a busy travel time for reasons such as family vacations, holidays and time off from work. This can be especially true for flights to Orlando, as summertime is one of the busiest seasons for Disney.

Disney, and other leisure travel destinations, see an increase in flight prices during the summer months. Flying during the off seasons will not only help you save money while at Disney, but on your flights as well.

THE BEST TIMES TO PURCHASE FLIGHTS FOR CHEAP AIRFARE

Cheapair.com completed an excellent study on the best times to book flights. In it, they analyzed over 4.1 million trips and fares to determine when ticket prices were the lowest. The booking window was 320 days to one day in advance for those 4.1 million trips, which resulted in **1.3 billion examined fares.** Talk about a number crunch!

FRUGAL TIP

SOUTHWEST WILL GIVE YOU A REFUND IF YOUR FARE DROPS IN PRICE! YOU CAN EVEN CHANGE YOUR FLIGHTS FOR FREE.

`Results showed that the "best day" to book flights was, on average, **54 days in advance or 7.5 weeks out.** That's just a general guideline, and there are many more variables to take into account from their study.

The following are general guidelines to follow when searching for airfare:

- The best booking window is **29-104 days out from your travel date.**

- **Flying in/out on Tuesdays to Thursdays** generally results in lower rates than most other days of the week.

- If you intend to travel during peak travel times, such as holidays and summer, you may need to consider booking your flight further in advance than you would otherwise (8+ weeks).

- If you know that you're going to be traveling far enough in advance, you should watch flight fares on a regular basis **starting about 100 days out. This will give you an idea of the 'good' rates.** Once you find one that you are comfortable with, jump on it! It will likely change soon.

- Booking too far in advance, more than 100 days out, could lead to more expensive airfares.

- **Consider flying out of other nearby airports** that might have much lower fares. If you live in the New York area, for example, you have many airport options available such as JFK, Newark and LaGuardia. The Philadelphia and Atlantic City airports are also not too long of a drive away.

FLIGHT PRICE TRACKING TOOLS

Many flight aggregation sites, like Kayak.com and Google Flights, provide you with a fare history on the flights you search for. This information is highly valuable because it can help you see if the fare for the particular flight you're searching is currently on the high side or the low side.

Kayak.com also provides predictions on how and when the flight fares will fluctuate in order to advise you on the best time(s) to purchase them. I frequently take advantage of Kayak's price alert emails feature. If you sign up, Kayak will send you email updates regarding changes in fares on a daily or weekly basis. That way, you can always be aware of the most up-to-date fares and, if you choose to, make a purchase before they change again.

The only downside to Kayak, and many other flight search sites, is that they do not include Southwest flights. For those, you will have to check Southwest.com.

HIDDEN CITY FLIGHTS

I'm going to tell you about a "secret" that airlines probably don't want you to know.

Let's face it: Airlines constantly try to sneak in those nickel and dime fees that can make the overall price of flying so much more than the initial base fares given. Anytime we can find a way to get around those while staying within the rules, of course, I'm all for it.

You may or may not have heard about hidden city fares, which is a special strategy to finding cheap airfares. In order to understand hidden city fares, you must first understand the primary rule of airline ticket pricing: Airline ticket prices are **based on competition**, not on distance flown.

Flights from my home city of Philadelphia are a good example of this. A flight from Philadelphia to Washington, which takes about 45 minutes and covers 300 or so miles, is running around $500 for a round-trip ticket. On the other hand, a flight from Philadelphia to Los Angeles, which takes six hours and covers 3,000 miles, is currently only around $365 for a round-trip ticket.

How can a flight that is 10 times longer be $135 cheaper? The answer is simple: because of competition.

American Airlines currently has no competition on their Philadelphia to Washington D.C. route, which is why they have the liberty to charge as they please for that flight. If you want to fly to D.C. from Philadelphia, you have no choice but to pay the highly marked-up fare. On the other hand, many airlines fly from Philadelphia to Los Angeles. You have several options for that route, but airlines still want you to pick them, which causes costs of those flights to drop.

In an attempt to undercut competitors, airlines will often price their direct flights higher than flights with connections. This is where the hidden city fares can come into play. As an example, let's take a look at flights between Charlotte, North Carolina, and Orlando, Florida. American Airlines operates a hub out of Charlotte, and they have the only option for a direct flight to there from Orlando.

With no competition on the route, American Airlines can charge whatever they want. Fares are usually in the $400+ range, even though it is a fairly short flight. For example, this one-way trip from Orlando to Charlotte pictured above is a whopping $449!

Now, if we were to add a connection to a "hidden city," we could potentially get a much lower price. Skiplagged.com specilizes in hidden city fares. By using their site, you can see that adding a connection in a "hidden city" such as Philadelphia **causes the fare to drop by hundreds of dollars!**

Our $449 flight has now dropped to $68, giving us **an incredible savings of $381!**

Why?

More competition between airlines exists on flights from Orlando to Philadelphia, so that route is priced lower. Skiplagged helps us find the hidden city fares that turn our final destination into a layover.

If we buy this ticket, we just won't get on that second flight to Philadelphia!

Just in case this is a little confusing, I'll break it down step by step:

1. Book a one-way flight from your current city to your final destination. If you're going to Disney World, that will be Orlando. Hidden city fares tend to work better on return flights from Orlando than on outgoing flights to Orlando.

2. When searching for your return flight, use skiplagged.com to search for a hidden city fare.

3. Book directly on the airline's website, not through travel portals like Orbitz.com. Having a third party involved can cause complications.

4. Your itinerary will now show that you have a connection in your home city. **Simply don't get on the last flight.**

The savings from using a hidden city fare can vary greatly and, for some cities, it might not even work. Generally, this works better if you live in or near a city that has an airport with an airline hub. If you're flying out from a small airport, you probably won't be able to take advantage of this.

If you find that you're able to use a hidden city fare, below are a few rules to follow that will make the process go smoothly:

1. **Don't check a bag.** If you do check bags, they will automatically continue on to your final destination city. **Only bring a carry-on bag.**

2. **Don't enter your frequent flyer number** when booking a hidden city fare. This is just to be on the safe side and avoid having airlines try to take any miles back.

3. **Be aware of itinerary changes**. If it changes at all, you might need to cancel or adjust flights to make sure your "connection" is still to your home airport.

4. **Always book on the airline's website**. Don't go through sites like Orbitz or Expedia because using third-party sites for hidden city fares can cause complications.

Although this trick may seem like a lot of work, as long as you follow these suggestions and make sure it's worth the price before purchasing, you could easily save a few hundred dollars on a flight.

FREE FLIGHTS USING
FREQUENT FLYER MILES

If you're only going to pay attention to a single section in this book, make it this one. The following tips on how to get free flights using your frequent flyer miles have the ability to **easily save you thousands of dollars on your next Disney vacation**.

Before we get into the details, let me first share my own story of using frequent flyer miles.

DISNEY FUN FACT
DISNEY OPENED A SMALL, PRIVATE AIRPORT ON THE PROPERTY IN 1971 AS A PROOF OF CONCEPT FOR A LARGER SCALE AIRPORT. THOSE PLANS WERE LATER REJECTED DUE TO NOISE AND COST CONCERNS.

Back in 2012, I was browsing Facebook when I came across an article posted on Gizmodo.com about someone who was able to fly around the world for only $400. My initial reaction was to think that they must have hitchhiked or used some sort of scam. I'm sure I wasn't alone in my reaction.

However, the article went on to explain how this person was able to get himself a round-the-world ticket through United Airlines by only using credit card sign-up bonuses.

That simple article changed my life.

Since then, I have been using this strategy to fly all over the world for pennies on the dollar. This has included many trips to Orlando. I've been able to use my frequent flyer miles to travel all over Europe and the United States, as well as to Thailand, Singapore, Mexico, Bali and Hawaii. I've also helped friends and family go on honeymoons and dream trips using free frequent flyer miles obtained through credit card sign-ups.

You might be thinking to yourself, *"This won't work because I'm not a frequent flyer."* Just give me a chance to explain how **you will never have to set foot on a plane to get enough miles for free flights.**

The strategy for this is actually fairly straightforward:

- Apply for credit cards that give frequent flyer miles as sign-up bonuses.
- Spend the required amount on that credit card to be awarded the free miles. This amount varies from card to card. Some don't require you to spend anything.
- Use the miles from the credit card bonus for free flights.

- Close the card.
- Rinse and repeat.

The two questions I'm most frequently asked about this process are:

1. **Won't this hurt my credit score?**
   Overall, no. The bank will do a hard pull of your credit score, also called an inquiry, when you apply for credit cards. This shows up on your credit report and can lower your score two to five points. However, the additional credit you'll now have available will offset that small drop and cause your score to go back up those two to five points. This will essentially leave your score unchanged. I have been doing this for years, and my credit score has consistently remained at 780+.

2. **Is doing this illegal or breaking the rules?**
   Not at all. There is absolutely nothing illegal about this, and it is not against any rules. We're not even bending any rules. Every suggestion outlined in this section falls within the rules of the credit card and airline companies.

BRIEF HISTORY ON FREQUENT FLYER PROGRAMS

Before we jump into the details of how to do this, perhaps it would help to give some background on frequent flyer programs, their purpose and how we can use them for our benefit.

A frequent flyer program is also known as a loyalty program. It is similar to, say, if you go to Starbucks and get a punch card to use every time you make a purchase. If you stay loyal to Starbucks and buy enough of their products to use up your punch card, you'll be awarded with a free drink.

Companies use loyalty programs as a way of giving their customers a reason to come back and continue using their products or services in the long term. It is often easier for companies to keep existing customers than it is for them to find new ones. This is no different from any airline's frequent flyer program: If you travel enough miles on a particular airline, they'll reward your loyalty with a free flight. The more you fly and spend money on an airline, the more free flights you'll be able to earn.

Earlier, I mentioned that you will never have to set foot on a plane to earn thousands of frequent flyer miles. You can use credit card sign-up bonuses instead. Credit card companies and airlines partner together to offer branded credit cards that extend the airline's loyalty program to your wallet. If you're an American Airlines AAdvantage member, why not get the AAdvantage credit card to earn miles for spending money?

HOW TO GET MILES

Let's take a look at the step-by-step process of getting frequent flyer miles through credit card sign-up bonuses. Southwest Airlines is one of my favorite airlines to use when I fly to Orlando. For this example, I'm going to use their frequent flyer program called Rapid Rewards.

Southwest Airlines is one of the best options to fly to Orlando.
Plus - checked bags are free!

I'm a huge fan of Southwest Airlines for a number of reasons:

•   **No Baggage Fees**: Unlike most other airlines, your first two bags fly free on Southwest. This alone can save you hundreds of dollars.

•   **Good Route Network**: You can fly to Orlando from just about any major city, which means they have very competitive rates when compared with other airlines.

•   **Simple Frequent Flyer Program**: Rapid Rewards is a very easy program to understand and use for redeeming miles. Unlike other airlines, you can use points on any flight. There are no blackouts and no low-level rewards.

- **Cheap Award Mile Redemptions**: Related to the above statement, the points needed for an award flight are tied to the price of the ticket. All other airlines charge 25,000 points per person regardless of ticket cost. With Southwest miles, you can get to Orlando for much less.

I've always had positive experiences on Southwest flights: Flight attendants are always friendly, the planes are new and clean, and you get to choose your own seats. It's definitely a no-frills airline, but it will get you to Orlando at a decent price so you can get your vacation started.

Below are the steps to obtain frequent flyer miles through credit card sign-up bonuses.

STEP 1: KNOW YOUR CREDIT SCORE

Your credit is one of the most important assets in your financial life. Having good credit will open up doors, such as credit card sign-up bonuses, as well as save you a lot of money in the long term through better interest rates.

Lenders will always want to make sure that the money they loan you will be paid back. Lending entities include credit card companies, mortgage companies and car dealerships. Before loaning you money, they will always check your credit score. This is how they judge your likelihood and ability to pay them back. A high credit score, in general, means that you pay your bills on time and take care of your finances. The higher your credit score, the higher your chances are of receiving a loan. The same is true when applying for credit cards.

If you don't know your credit score, you can check it at MyFico.com. If you're a first-time member, you can check your score for free.

In order to be able to apply for travel credit cards that will give you frequent flyer miles, you need to have a credit score of 700 or higher.

If you're at 700 or above, congrats! You have good credit and can move on to the next step. If your score is under 700, you're not quite ready to move on in this process. You need to get that score up first! I would suggest using the tools on the MyFico site to see why your score is under 700. Is it because of late bills? Is your credit utilization too high? Do you have any accounts out for collections? Is there a mistake on your credit report?

Once you get your score over 700, you'll be able to to continue with this process.

STEP 2: OBTAIN AND USE CREDIT CARD SIGN-UP BONUSES

Congratulations - your credit score is high enough to begin the next step of getting to Disney for pennies on the dollar!

The Barry family's goal is to accumulate enough frequent flyer miles for them to get four round-trip tickets to Orlando on Southwest. Instead of spending a lot of money and buying many flights to earn these miles, we are going to explore the easy, free route: **credit card sign-up bonuses.**

Companies that sell airline-branded credit cards give away large numbers of airline miles as an incentive to sign up for and use these cards. In return for hitting spending limits, you are rewarded with a number of airline miles. The bonuses and required spending amounts vary with each card.

Why Do Airlines Do This? **You might think that airlines lose money through their frequent flyer programs but, in reality, they actually rake in billions of dollars**.

I'll quickly explain.

Airlines want their planes to be full for each flight, and credit card companies want their cards to be swiped. By teaming up, credit card companies can purchase hundreds of millions of frequent flyer miles from various airlines. They can then give these away as an incentive for people to sign up for their cards, which they make money from. People then redeem those miles, which helps airlines keep their planes full. Airlines also have the ability to control both the "value" of their miles and when they expire.

Imagine if you had $1 in your wallet that would be worth 50 cents tomorrow because the government decided to change its value. Then, imagine if they said that the 50 cents in your wallet would expire after two years?

All in all, it's a pretty lucrative deal for both the airline and credit card companies. Even with these "free" flights, they are both still bringing in a lot of money for their businesses.

At the time this book was written, the best available credit card offer is the Chase Southwest Rapid Rewards credit card. After signing up **you'll**

receive 50,000 points after you spend $2,000 on the card within the first three months. The annual fee of $99 is not waived for the first year, so that is a cost that you'll have to pay for this card. Be sure to check http://www.frugalmouse.com/best-credit-card-deals/ for the latest and best credit card sign up offers.

You might be thinking, *"but there's a $99 annual fee!"*

Yes. A $99 fee is no fun to pay, and it will be included on your first statement every year. However, paying the annual $99 fee will allow you to get points that will ultimately save you hundreds of dollars on flights. The 50,000 point sign-up bonus is worth about **$600+ in free airfare.** When you subtract the annual fee, **you're still $500+ ahead.**

Rapid Rewards points are worth between **60 and 70 points per dollar** of the fare. For example, if a round-trip fare is $250, it will take about 17,500 Rapid Rewards points for a free flight ($250 x 70 = 17,500). The mandatory September 11 security fee of $2.50 is not included in the point redemption, so you'll have to pay that out of pocket.

Southwest actually doesn't release exact point-to-dollar ratios, which is why I'm giving ranges. It varies between flights. If you use the 60-70 points per dollar formula, you'll be able to estimate pretty close to the number of points needed.

Southwest's Rapid Rewards point system is is a great deal in the airline miles business because most other airlines charge 25,000 points for a round-trip flight within the U.S. at economy fare. That means that a round-trip flight to Orlando for a family of four would cost 100,000 points!

You're going to have **52,000+ points with Rapid Rewards**, which will get you about **$700 in free airfare on Southwest**. That's about $175 a person for a family of four, which probably won't be quite enough for most. Let's look at some ways to earn more points.

When you use your Southwest credit card, you earn one point per $1 spent. If you spend an average of $1,000 a month, you'll be getting an extra 1,000 Southwest miles each month for just spending money you would have spent anyway. I would suggest spending a little more with the card to get up to about 56,000 points, which will get you $800 in free airfare on Southwest.

Another option is to have your significant other apply for the same card. That would give you a combined 104,000 Southwest Rapid Rewards points, which is worth $1,485 in free flights.

Before applying for the credit card, you need to sign up for a Rapid Rewards account through Southwest.com. Keep your Rapid Rewards number handy because you'll need to provide that on your card application.

When the card(s) arrive, activate them by calling the number printed on them. For easy bill payment, I recommend setting up accounts online.

You're all set! It's now time to start working towards that $2,000 spendings requirement.

STEP 3 - HITTING THAT SPENDINGS REQUIREMENT

Now that you have your card in hand, you need to be sure to hit the spendings requirement of $2,000 within the first three months.

The golden rule of credit cards is that you should **only spend the amount that you can pay off IN FULL each month**. If you carry a balance, miss payments or only pay the minimum amount, you'll be hit with financing and other fees.

I recommend that you choose to pay the full statement balance each month and that you do that by setting up an automatic payment through your bank account. That way, there will be no risk of forgetting to pay. As long as you pay your statement balance in full each month, it will cost you nothing additional to earn points on your card.

If you are not able to control your spending or pay off each month in full, this method is not for you! You'll be charged extra fees. Don't give away your hard-earned money to the credit card companies. Have them pay you, in points, to use their cards!

Spending $2,000 in three months shouldn't be too difficult for a family of four. Every penny you spend can be placed on the card and then paid off each month. Examples of expenses you can put on your cards include:

- Groceries
- Cable/Internet
- Cell phone bills
- Dining out

- Gas
- Insurance
- Mortgage/car payments (watch out for added fees)

Another strategy I've used is purchasing Disney gift cards with the credit cards. If you do this, you're basically pre-paying for some of your Disney expenses and, at the same time, working to meet the minimum spendings requirements. Just be sure to keep your gift cards safe, and treat them as you would treat cash.

When Will I Get My Points?

You will see the points awarded to your account on the first statement you receive after passing the $2,000 spendings mark. If you provided a Rapid Rewards account number when you signed up for the card, these points will be placed in your Rapid Rewards account within a few weeks. If you didn't sign up for a Rapid Rewards account before opening your card, you'll be assigned one.

FRUGAL TIP
WHEN FLYING SOUTHWEST, BE SURE TO CHECK-IN TO YOUR FLIGHT EXACTLY 24 HOURS BEFORE DEPARTURE SO YOU CAN CHOOSE YOUR SEAT FIRST.

How to Get Even More Points

Another strategy to get even more Rapid Reward points, in addition to spending on the card, is to use the Rapid Reward Shopping Mall. If you frequently shop online, it's worth it to go through the Rapid Rewards Mall to earn even more points on your purchases online.

For example, if you shop on Nike.com through the Rapid Rewards Shopping Mall right now, you'll earn double points on all purchases. Let's say you purchased a $100 pair of sneakers from Nike. You'll earn double that amount in Rapid Rewards points, which is 200 points. If you put that purchase on your Southwest card, you'll earn another 100 points. In the end, you will earn a total of **300 Rapid Rewards points** on your $100 shoe purchase. Not bad at all!

STEP 4 - FINDING AWARD FLIGHTS

Fast forward three months to when you should have earned 52,000+ frequent flyer miles through Southwest without ever even leaving the ground! Think about it: If you actually were to fly 52,000 miles, you would have to fly across the country more than **17 times!**

Now that you have the points, it's time for the fun part - spending them! You'll use the same search method that you use for regular paid flights but, instead of paying cash, you'll use your Rapid Rewards points.

Let's head over to Southwest.com to find flights to Orlando. For this example, I'm going to use flights from Philadelphia (PHL) to Orlando International (MCO) for the Barry family's trip in May.

You'll need to have flexibility in your schedule when redeeming points for flights. Certain days will have cheaper flights, which means fewer miles are needed for those free flights. During your planning, I would recommend booking your airfare first. Then make sure those dates work with hotels.

Let's take a look at the search results for the Barry family's flight from Philadelphia to Orlando.

On this day, it looks like all flights are going for as low as 5,137 to just 8,327 points which is quite the bargain! Just to be sure, I always check Southwest's low fare calendar to find the lowest fares. This will equate to the lowest number of points needed.

Departing Flight: Philadelphia, PA to Orlando, FL

SHOW FARES IN
○ $ ● POINTS

First 2 Bags Fly Free®. Weight, size & excess limits apply.

Award travel is subject to payment of the government-imposed September 11th Security Fee, of $5.60 per one-way trip.

Jan | Feb | Mar | Apr | **May** | Jun | Jul | Aug | Now accepting reservations through August 5, 2016.

Sun	Mon	Tue	Wed	Thu	Fri	Sat
1 5,527	2 5,137	3 5,137	4 5,137	5 7,025	6 5,364	7 5,364
8 8,327	9 5,137	10 5,137	11 5,527	12 8,327	13 8,327	14 7,025
15 5,527	16 5,137	17 5,137	18 5,137	19 7,025	20 7,025	21 7,025
22 5,527	23 5,527	24 5,137	25 5,527	26 8,327	27 9,629	28 7,025
29 7,025	30 8,327	31 5,137				

Show Me:
☑ Business Select Starting at 53,568
☑ Anytime Starting at 42,593
☑ Wanna Get Away Starting at 5,137

Update Calendar

Based on the low fare calendar, our best bets are to fly down to Orlando sometime between a Monday and a Wednesday, which is pretty common. Flying Thursdays through Saturdays, which are more popular days to travel, will generally cost us more points. Remember that this is only the outbound flight: You will have to select the inbound flight on the next screen.

Depart	Arrive	Flight #	Routing	Travel Time	Business Select 53,568 Pts	Anytime 42,593 Pts	Wanna Get Away from 5,690 Pts
7:00 AM	9:25 AM	2239	Nonstop	2h 25m	53,568	42,593	7,676
9:00 AM	11:25 AM	2234	Nonstop	2h 25m	53,568	42,593	7,676
11:15 AM	1:40 PM	3673	Nonstop	2h 25m	53,568	42,593	5,723
6:10 PM	8:50 PM	1670	Nonstop	2h 40m	53,568	42,593	7,676

To reduce total travel time and the possibility of missing a connection, I always start by looking at non-stop flights. If your city doesn't have any direct flights, this option won't be available. I like getting down to Orlando nice and early, so I would go with the 7 a.m. or 8:40 a.m. flights. Per person, this would cost just over 10,000 points for a round-trip ticket.

You'll also see Business Select and Anytime point options. I would avoid these because they're very expensive and don't come with enough perks to make them worth the cost.

Finally, just add in the total mandatory fees of $20 and the annual fee of $99. **The total cost per person for a family of four to fly to Orlando is $29.75!** That's **$119 total** for all four members of the family.

Just How Much Could You Save on Flights?

In this example, the total cash cost of these flights would be $733.60. By using points, the Barry family could get them for a total of $119 after the added mandatory fees and annual $99 card payment. That's a **grand total savings of $614.60.** Later, we'll get into the details of the Barry family's final decision.

Shaving over $600 off the cost of a vacation puts it in reach for many families. It also could allow you to stay longer, buy the kids a few extra souvenirs or take more frequent trips.

In summary, Southwest offers a great frequent flyer program for domestic travel called Rapid Rewards. They also have a lot of flights to Orlando from many cities around the country. In order to travel to Orlando on Southwest for free, you'll have to earn enough frequent flyer miles. I hope that by using your Chase Southwest credit cards, along with the other suggestions above, you are able to successfully fly your family to Disney as cheaply as possible.

To recap, here is the step-by-step process you'll need to follow to get free flights using frequent flier miles.

1. As soon as you know the date of your trip (or at least 6 months out), apply for the mileage earning credit card.

2. Over the next three months put all spending on the card to satisfy the spending requirement. Pay the card off in full each month!

3. As soon as you have the miles in your account, begin looking for award flights for the dates of your trip.

4. When you find the right flight, book it using your miles!

SAVING MONEY ON RENTAL CARS

The reality for many of us is that we live too far away to be able to drive to Orlando. Unless we are staying at a Disney resort on-site, which would allow us to take advantage of Disney's Magical Express bus service, we'll have to rent a car when we arrive at MCO.

Many families stay off-site in order to save money by keeping hotel costs down. However, this also adds the need for a rental car. The cost of that car could, potentially, negate those hotel savings. Car rental companies don't make it easy to find deals, especially at high leisure-locations like Orlando.

Just about every car rental company is represented at the Orlando International Airport, which creates a lot of competition between them and can really lower prices. Doing just a little bit of research on this, which we will cover in this section, can save you hundreds of dollars on your rental car.

There are many sites that allow you to find very cheap rental cars. Priceline is a great example. Priceline.com has a bidding feature that allows you to "name your own price" on rental cars. This gives you the opportunity to get deep discounts on rentals. The only problem is that the Priceline rental car bidding system has many rules, which can make it confusing for users. I'll show you, step by step, how to use Priceline to your advantage and find the best deal on a rental car.

HOW PRICELINE.COM WORKS

Priceline allows you to use two different methods when booking cars. The first is the standard "search" option, which pulls slightly-discounted, published rates. Generally, you'll be able to find these rates on either the rental car company's website or other search sites.

The second option is to "name your own price," which is their term for bidding on rental cars. We'll get into how this works a little further down in this section.

When rental car companies have unbooked cars or are forecasting that there will be less rentals at certain times, they will go to sites like Priceline. com and post their cars at very discounted rates. Of course, the rental car companies don't want to advertise these low rates because there is always a chance that renters won't look at Priceline and will still book cars at retail rates. This is why you won't see the name of the car company until you've actually booked your rental.

So now that you know how Priceline.com works, how exactly do you go about getting your rental car for a bargain? Follow the steps below.

1. RESEARCH PRICELINE RENTAL CAR BIDDING

Before bidding for cars on Priceline, your first order of business is always to do a little research and find some of the recent winning bids on cars. This will help you get an idea of where to start bidding, as well as help you make sure to get the absolute best deal possible for your car.

My favorite site to go to for this is called Biddingfortravel.com, which is dedicated to helping people get the best bids on Priceline.com and other similar sites. This site can also be used to see recent winning hotel bids in certain cities, but we'll be looking primarily at the car rental section for this example.

Let's go to the Orlando rental cars section to get an idea of some recently successful bids.

When taking a glance through the forums, you can see from the screenshot above that rentals in May for an SUV have gone for $15 a day up to

Boyle County Public Library

$30 a day. Your goal is to locate a bid that was accepted on a class of car similar to what you want and that was also within your desired rental time frame. This is what you'll use as a starting point for bidding on your rental car.

2. BID FOR YOUR RENTAL CAR

After you have a price range in mind, you're ready to start the bidding process for your car. The real value that Priceline provides is the ability to name your own price by bidding for your car rentals. This will get you great rates, but it requires some work.

On the Priceline.com homepage, select the cars tab. You'll see the normal search area. You'll want to use the bidding feature, which will allow you to get even better discounts on rental cars.

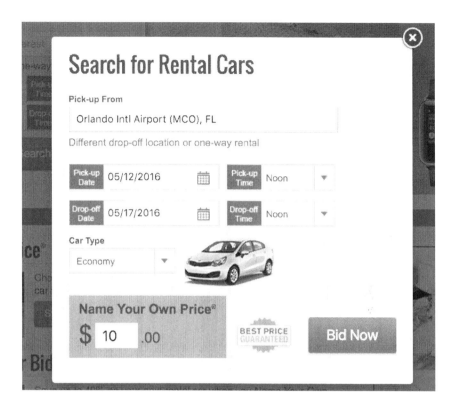

Enter all of the information about the location, along with the date and times that you'll need the car. (MCO = Orlando International Airport) **It is very important that you bid a price you know won't get accepted.** You should do this because you want to see what Priceline will suggest as a more reasonable bid. You'll use this information to help guide your bidding process.

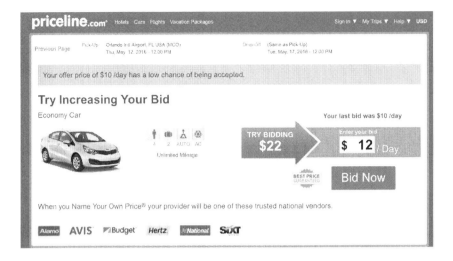

The next screen you'll see will be Priceline calling you "crazy." That $1/day isn't going to be accepted!

Why not, Priceline???

Why do they give a "suggested" bid that is clearly too high? This is where you'll use those prices we found on the Bidding for Travel forums. It looked like bids around $16/day were being accepted, so you could start there.

Summary of Charges

Your Offer Price:	**$16.00 (per day)**
Total Rental Days:	5
Subtotal:	**$80.00**
Taxes and Fees: (details)	**$54.30**
Total Charges: prices are in US dollars	**$134.30**

After you enter your bid, the next screen will ask for your payment information. Here are a few important notes to keep in mind before you move past this step:

- If your bid is accepted by a company, your card will be charged and the car will be booked. **There are no cancellations without a very hefty penalty.** Don't even try to beg Priceline - they won't hear it.

- Since there are no cancellations and changes allowed, **make sure to double-check that your dates are correct.**

- Before your bid is accepted, **you won't know which company you'll end up with**. That's ok. It'll be one of the major rental companies at Orlando International, so don't worry.

After you click submit, you'll see one of a several possible outcomes:

1. **Your bid was accepted**. If you see this, congrats! You just locked in a great deal on a rental car.

2. **Your bid wasn't accepted** because it was too low. I'll give you more on what to do with this result in a minute.

3. **You received a counter bid.** Generally, you will not want to accept these counter bids because they're probably not that great of a deal. If you find that it is a good deal, however, go ahead and accept it.

3. RE-BIDDING ON PRICELINE

In most cases, you'll end up with outcome #2. This is where the fun part comes in. The rules of Priceline state that you can only re-bid the exact same amount on a car every 24 hours. However, you can **simply switch the car type and bid amount and continue bidding**. For example, if I'm bidding $15/day on a standard car and that gets declined, I could try $13/day for a compact car or $16/day for a full-sized car.

If you choose to continue bidding, click "Bid On A Different Car" in the upper right hand corner of the page. You'll then be presented with a page that will allow you to continue bidding on different car types. This is shown below.

Take note of the bids that you're making for each car type. If your bids are not accepted, wait for 24 hours and then increase your bid amount by $1/day for each car type until it is accepted. That's what I usually do! Of course, don't bid on car types you don't want. Bid on the ones that you'd be comfortable ending up with.

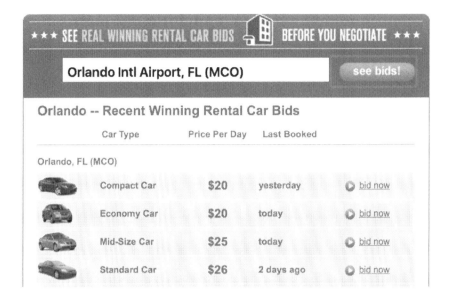

If you're unsuccessful during your first round, don't fret. You can just try again tomorrow when you'll be allowed a fresh start to bidding. It may take a couple of days before you finally get a bid accepted, but it'll be well worth the work. You'll wind up with a car for a much lower price than a retail rental would be. If you're like me, you'll welcome the extra research, work and persistence if the end result is a rental car at a 50 percent discount or higher!

FRUGAL TIP

BE SURE TO PURCHASE GAS AND FILL UP BEFORE GETTING NEAR THE AIRPORT WHERE PRICES ARE INFLATED.

Remember that things can change from day to day. If you bid $15 on a car today and get rejected, that same $15 might be accepted tomorrow. Continue to work on your bids, and check back to get that great deal on your car. Don't give up!

DRIVING TO DISNEY ON THE CHEAP

If you're one of the lucky ones who live close enough to Florida, driving to Orlando instead of flying could be a great and cheap alternative way to travel. Even if it would be somewhat of a long road trip, you could potentially save a lot of money. This is especially true if you have a larger family and can pack everyone into a large car or van.

If you choose to drive, gas prices will be one of your largest variables in terms of cost. Generally, gas prices will be higher during the summer because people tend to travel more during those months. Gas will also be slightly more expensive at stations along highways because of the convenience of their locations. For a longer trip, it's important that the vehicle you take gets great gas mileage. This will help you save money. Today, most new cars have a miles per gallon (mpg) indicator.

DISNEY FUN FACT
WALT DISNEY SPECIFICALLY CHOSE THE LOCATION OF WALT DISNEY WORLD BECAUSE OF IT'S EASY ACCESS TO I-4 AND CLOSE PROXIMITY TO THE ORLANDO INTERNATIONAL AIRPORT.

To give you an idea on how much money you'll need to budget for gas, calculate your estimated gas prices before you leave. For example, let's say your car averages 29 mpg on the highway and your round-trip mileage is 1,500 miles. Gas prices fluctuate regularly so, for this example, let's assume the average is $2.70/gallon.

1,500 miles / 29 mpg = 51.72 gallons. Let's round this up to 52. This is the total gallons of gas you'll need for your trip. 52 gallons x $2.70 per gallon = $140.40. This is the estimated cost of gas for your whole trip.

To be on the safe side, I would budget around $175 for gas. If you find yourself spending a lot more money on gas than expected, you might have a gas mileage problem that you want to look into.

You will also need to take into account the cost of a hotel room for a night if you need to stop during your drive down. It's better to be safe and spend a night rather than drive drowsy!

How Can You Make Your Car More Gas Efficient?
Optimizing your car to ensure you're getting the most possible miles per gallon out of it will help save you money during your road trip. Below are a few tips that you can easily use to help make your car more fuel efficient:

- **Properly inflate your tires.** This is possibly the most important tip. Make sure your tires are inflated to their proper air pressure before starting your trip. For most cars, that means a PSI of 30-35. Be sure to double check your car's proper inflation levels in the car manual. Be sure to check, even during your trip (on cold tires), so that you're not losing any air.

- **Clean your air filter.** Your engine needs to suck in air in order to operate properly. If it's being restricted by a clogged or dirty air filter, you'll be losing precious mpgs. Before you leave on your trip, replace your air filter. It's only a few dollars for a new one, which you will more than make up for in gas savings.

- **Put your car on a diet.** The harder your engine has to work, the less efficient it will be. If you have items in your car that don't need to be there, remove them before leaving on your trip. Pack light. You can always do laundry while at your resort. A lighter car is a more efficient car.

- **Drive at night**. This has both pros and cons. The cons are that you might be tired while driving at night, and it might not be enjoyable for you and your family because you won't get to see any of the landscapes or scenery you're passing by. The pros of driving at night, however, are less traffic and cooler temperatures that will help your car operate more efficiently.

- **Drive at a constant speed.** Rapid acceleration takes up more gas, and hard braking wears out your brakes more quickly. If you're usually an aggressive driver, try to avoid doing these things because they can make your trip more expensive. You'll maximize your fuel efficiency by keeping your speed as consistent as possible through light acceleration and light braking. Using cruise control is a great way to help with this. The ideal speed to travel on the highway is around 60 to 65 mph. Going faster than that can increase wind drag, which hurts your gas mileage.

- **Avoid traffic jams.** You can use an app called Waze that will alert you to traffic jams ahead in your route. That way, you have the option of rerouting before it's too late. I use this app often. Nothing is worse than sitting for hours in traffic!

- **Pack food for the car ride.** Not only will packing food for the trip save you money, but it will also save you time by reducing the overall number of stops you'll need to take. I always pack snacks and a cooler of drinks to have in the car.

Before going on long road trips, I always like to take my car to my mechanic for a check up. You want to make sure the most important things are in proper working order: brakes, tires, suspension and oil.

A car break down or mechanical malfunction halfway down I-95 could really put a damper on your vacation.

RIDING THE RAILS

So far, I've covered automobile and air travel options for your trip to Disney. This next section is about traveling by train. To be completely honest, I have never taken the train myself and don't really recommend taking Amtrak. Here are my reasons:

- Over long distances, trains are usually no faster than driving by yourself. For example, the train from Philadelphia to Orlando takes 19 hours. I've easily made that drive in 15-16 hours.

- In almost all cases, trains are more expensive than driving. Sometimes they're even equal to or more expensive than flying!

- Train routes and schedules are much more limited than the options you have with flights.

I do know some people who take the train and really enjoy the experience - it is nice to not have to worry about driving. Maybe you're a train enthusiast like them. If that's the case, taking a train could add to the overall enjoyment and experience of your trip.

In general, I still have a hard time recommending the train over flying or driving. If you use the tips above to score a discounted or free flight, you'll get there faster and cheaper than you would if you took a train. Trains are always more expensive than driving. I have yet to find a fare on Amtrak that would cost me less to get to Florida than driving would.

If you take a train, you'll also be without a car once you arrive. (Unless you take the Amtrak Auto train, which is very expensive.) So you'll have to rent a car or rely on cabs and Disney transportation to get around.

With all that being said, I don't want to completely discourage anyone from looking into Amtrak as an option. If you live near a station, I'd say it's worth exploring. Maybe it will work in your particular case!

HOW THE BARRYS ARE GETTING TO ORLANDO

Now that we're all equipped with this new information on how to get to Orlando cheaply, let's see just how much more money the Barrys can save on their trip.

Their minivan gets about 27 mpg on the highway, which equates to around $200 in gas and 32 total hours in the car if they choose to drive. They live in Philadelphia, which means it would take them approximately 16 hours to drive to Orlando. This is more than anyone in the family wants to spend in a car.

Flying sounds much more appealing to the whole family, as it's only a two-hour flight from PHL to MCO and they'll have many time options to choose from for their flight.

Mom Barry also applied for the Southwest credit card, which earned her 52,000 points after she paid the $99 annual fee and fulfilled the $2,000 spendings requirement. Those 52,000 miles are more than enough to fly their family of four to Orlando.

When looking at flight options, Mom Barry found that the cheapest option is $250/person for a round-trip ticket arriving in Orlando on May 15 and departing on May 19. This includes all taxes and fees. Multiply that by four people, and they end up with a total ticket cost of $1,000. This a large amount of money. As mentioned at the beginning of this chapter, the Barrys can't afford to spend this much on flights.

The total cost in Southwest points for those same flights comes to 10,470 points + $11.20 for taxes/fees per person. This is a total of 41,880 points + $44.80 for all four members of their family. They can't forget about that $99 annual fee they had to pay for their credit card. So the grand total, when using points, is 41,880 points + $143.80.

The original cost of their tickets, without points, was $1,000. $1,000 - $143.80 = **a savings of $856.20!** Even after redeeming for these flights, the Barrys will still have a little over 10,000 miles that can be used for a future trip.

Flying a family of four to Orlando for an out-of-pocket cost of $143.80 ($35.95/person) is simply an amazing deal that is almost impossible to beat. It even comes out cheaper than driving the family car, and it's definitely quite a bit faster.

If the Barry family did happen to decide to drive, the total cost in gas for the trip would be around $200. That isn't bad at all. To make the drive more enjoyable, they could plan to make several stops and see some sights along the way. Perhaps the biggest "cost" to driving is the amount of time it takes, which many people are perfectly ok with!

After the Barrys arrive in Orlando, they'll need to rent a car to get them to their resort and some off-site restaurants. After searching through some of the car search aggregation sites such as Kayak.com, they found that the average prices are between $22 and $30, depending on the class of car chosen.

The Barrys are just a family of four, but they will still need to put a good amount of luggage in their trunk. In renting a car, they decided to go with with a mid-sized car that will allow for a little more space. With cars at $25/day on average, that adds up to $125 for a five-day trip. When we include the $25 for taxes/fees, we get a total of $150.

All of the tips and strategies outlined in this chapter can be applied to any type of travel: from trips to Europe or a simple car ride to grandma's house.

Everything is in the context of a Disney trip because we are focusing on Disney in this book. However, if you have a family trip to San Francisco or somewhere else in the future - look into booking your flights with points!

PARK TICKETS

Park admission tickets likely will be one of the biggest expenses for your trip to Disney World. The opportunity to experience all the rides, shows, parades and other attractions the parks provide is largely why we go in the first place. Who would want to pass that up? We can't get enough!

Unfortunately, our love for Disney is reflected in their ticket prices. Disney knows that most of us will be willing to pay the premium they charge for a full park experience, so finding discounts on tickets is no easy task.

Navigating the maze of Disney park tickets can leave your head spinning. Between all of the options, vendors, packages and specials available, you could spend days trying to get the best deal. I'm here to help you save yourself a lot of time and, hopefully, money by simply outlining the best options for discount tickets that you can find right now.

Before we dive into some of these money-saving tips, let's take an in-depth look at all of your Disney park and ticket options.

What You Will Learn in this Chapter:

- How Disney prices tickets to make them sound like a great deal
- Tips to prevent you from getting scammed
- What the cheapest park ticket options are
- Is park hopping worth the cost?
- All about the "Water Parks Fun & More" option

PARK ADMISSION TICKET PRICING

Disney offers park admission tickets, called Magic Your Way tickets, in the form of the total number of days you want to visit. This can be anywhere from single-day passes to annual passes that are valid for a full year (365 days). Most visitors will purchase tickets in the 3- to 7-day range, which grants access into a park from opening to closing for that full number of days.

Once you have your ticket in hand - time to start the fun!

Disney structures the pricing of their tickets in a very interesting and somewhat deceiving way. The more days that you add to your park ticket, the cheaper each day gets. Take a look at the chart below.

Number of Days	Cost	Price Per Day
1	$97* - $124*	$97* - $124*
2	$192	$96
4	$305	$76.25
7	$335	$47.86
10	$365	$36.50

* 1-Day ticket prices vary based on season and the park.
Front and center on Disney's ticket website, you'll notice that prices are broken down by individual day. This makes it seem a lot cheaper to purchase tickets of a longer duration. Don't fall into the trap.

As you can see from the table above, the price per day reduces drastically as you get into the 4+ day tickets. This makes those longer tickets seem like a much better deal. However, it's important to keep in mind that, even though you're paying less per day for your park ticket, you'll also need to multiply your food and hotel costs by the extra number of days. Usually, this will negate the ticket discounts.

In 2016, Disney introduced seasonal pricing for their single-day park tickets. The calendar is broken down into three different seasons: value, regular and peak. Each season prices single-day park tickets differently. Take a look at the chart below for the pricing breakdowns per season.

Season	Magic Kingdom	Epcot, Hollywood Studios, Animal Kingdom
Value	$105	$97
Regular	$110	$102
Peak	$124	$114

The dates for each season are going to be variable, so I would check on Disney's official website for dates of each season. As a general rule of thumb, the seasons are broken down as follows:

Value
- End of August
- September
- January (except New Years)
- February

Regular
- April
- May (except Memorial Day weekend)
- First three weeks of August
- October
- November (except Thanksgiving week)
- Beginning of December

Peak
- Middle to the end of March (Spring Break)
- June
- July (except for last week)
- Thanksgiving week

- Christmas week

These are the seasons at the time this book was published, these dates can and will change.

Based on the ticket pricing, the best value for your time and money are park tickets between the 4- to 6-day time range. Why? This gives you enough time to hit all of the parks and even have a chance to go back and see some of your favorites with the extra days. That range of days falls between $54 to $76 per day, which I think is very reasonable.

DISNEY FUN FACT
WHEN THE MAGIC KINGDOM OPENED IN 1971, THE COST OF AN ADMISSION TICKET WAS ONLY $3.50!

You'll rarely ever see a total ticket price online or in the parks at the ticket kiosks. You'll always see the prices listed per day, which makes the offer appear to be a great deal. I've found that many people seem to underestimate the total cost of park tickets, which is understandable because of the way Disney displays the prices. To illustrate this, if I were to read you the two sentences below, which option would sound cheaper?

- We're going to Disney, and it will cost $76 per person per day for four days.
- We're going to Disney, and it will cost us $1,220 in park tickets.

Of course the $76 per day sounds much cheaper. However, in reality, both prices are equal.

Remember: As you're doing the math for your trip, be sure to take the time to add up all of the costs. Don't assume the discounted Disney tickets will make things cheaper overall.

The Barrys would like to hit all four of the big parks during their trip, which includes Magic Kingdom, Epcot, Hollywood Studios and Animal Kingdom.

They also would like to have the flexibility to hop between parks, which means they will need a hopper option added to their tickets. Initially, they think they should go with a 4-day park hopper pass. This will allow them to hit at least one park a day and includes the opportunity to hop between parks as they choose.

Tommorowland is my favorite land at the Magic Kingdom.
Which land is your favorite?

For their family of four, the Barry family's total ticket cost will be $1,571.96. This is a big portion of their overall vacation budget. In fact, this will actually be the single largest expense for their trip. We'll need to work hard to try to get this cost down. That is the price directly from Disney, so let's dive in and see how the Barry family can shave off some costs!

DISNEY WORLD TICKET BUYING TIPS

There are a few rules you should take into account when purchasing your park tickets. You'll probably be spending a good chunk of your vacation budget on tickets, so let's make sure you're getting the best deal possible.

1. **Purchase as early as you can.** As history has shown, it's not a matter of **if** Disney will raise their park ticket prices, but **when** they will raise them. The saying goes that the only things certain in life are death and taxes. Let's add an increase in Disney park tickets to that list.

   Disney has consistently raised park ticket prices for years now, so it should be expected that they'll continue that trend. In order to avoid the price hikes as much as possible, park tickets should be the first purchase you make as soon as you know that you will be going on a vacation to Disney World.

2. **Only purchase tickets from authorized sellers.** Do not, I repeat, **do not purchase tickets off of eBay, Craigslist or any similar sites!** I've heard too many stories of people getting ripped off. Being scammed out of thousands of dollars on fake or used tickets will not be a fun experience for you or your family. To avoid this, stick with official Disney park ticket sellers. Disney themselves, AAA/CAA and the Official Ticket Center are a few examples. Most Disney area hotels also have a ticket window at their front desks that sells park tickets. Just double check that they are official. As long as you stick with the official ticket providers, you won't run the risk of falling victim to a scam. I know those cheap tickets on eBay look enticing, but it's not worth the risk.

3. **Make a copy of your tickets.** This is a very important one. After you receive your physical tickets, be sure to **make a photocopy or take a picture of the front and back of your tickets.** If your tickets were to be lost or stolen, having the information on a copy as proof of purchase will be the only way for you to get a replacement. I always scan a copy of my tickets, as well as print out a physical copy to bring along with us on the trip. I also take a picture of the tickets with my iPhone to have a backup copy, just in case. **Treat your tickets just like cash!**

Cheapest Park Ticket Options Right Now

The list of options below includes your best options for purchasing Disney park tickets at a discount right now.

Official Ticket Resellers

Official Disney park ticket resellers like Undercover Tourist and The Official Ticket Center are licensed by Disney to sell their park tickets, and they can provide great deals. How do they get discounted tickets to sell? Well, they receive excess tickets that are not sold by Disney and then sell them at a discount to the public.

FRUGAL TIP

DISNEY RAISES TICKET PRICES EVERY YEAR. IT'S NOT A MATTER OF IF, BUT A MATTER OF WHEN. AS SOON AS YOU KNOW YOU'RE GOING, BUY YOUR TICKETS RIGHT AWAY TO AVOID THE PRICE HIKES.

Generally, these are some of the cheapest prices that you will find on Disney park tickets. All of **their tickets are Fastpass+ enabled,** so you can take advantage of the Fastpass+ system.

You can even get a better discount on Undercover Tourist tickets if you sign up for the Mousesavers.com newsletter, which includes a discount code each month for an additional 15 percent off park tickets.

The Tree of Life In Animal Kingdom has over 300 animals carved into its trunk.

One of the more popular tickets, the 5-Day Magic Your Way with park hopper, is currently going for $413 on Undercover Tourist. Disneyworld.com has the same exact ticket for $435. With Undercover Tourist, you'll be saving $22 or about a 6 percent discount, which is not bad at all.

Different tickets types have varying levels of discounts available, so take a look at the number of days and options you'll be needing and compare the prices.

AAA/CAA Discounts

Through their various regional branches, auto clubs AAA and CAA sometimes offer discounted Disney World tickets or discount packages that include tickets. There generally isn't too much of a discount to be had with these auto clubs, but you do get other perks like discounts, special parking and lounges to hang out in.

To find deals in your area, check our your local AAA/CAA branch.

SHOULD I PARK HOP?

During my travels to Disney, I started noticing that a lot of people, including myself, were purchasing the costly park hopper option for their tickets. This option allows you to enter any of the four parks as many times you want during that day. You can hop from park to park as much as you wish.

I love park hopping, and I know I'm not alone in that! I've actually done all four parks in one day. Talk about a lot of commuting! It was both a fun and exhausting day. I really enjoy being able to hit Magic Kingdom in the morning, head over to Hollywood Studios to view the early Fantasmic, then hop over to Epcot to end the night with Illuminations. Sounds like the perfect day to me.

Up until very recently, I purchased the park hopper option just about every trip. After looking at the costs, I started wondering – **Is it really worth it?**

Park hopping does give you a lot of flexibility. It sure is fun being able to go to the Magic Kingdom early and hit the mountain ranges, then head to Epcot on the monorail to catch dinner, and then end the day with Illuminations.

Disney loves to offer this option on their tickets because it doesn't cost them anything. You're already paying for your base fare so, from their end, it doesn't matter whether you go to one or six parks in a day.

There are some things to consider before buying the park hopping option. We'll cover each of those below.

PARK HOPPING IS EXPENSIVE

Park hopping is an add-on that you can select when purchasing your base tickets. On top of the base price, Disney charges $69 per ticket for the ability to hop between parks.

For example, if I wanted a 4-day ticket with no hopping, my base price would be $325 total or $81.25/day. If I were to add the park hopping option, that price would go up to $394 total or $98.50/day. With tax, that adds up to an extra $63. For a family of four, **that would be an extra $276!**

Looking out over World Showcase lagoon at Epcot from the Japan pavilion.

Consistent with Disney's general ticket pricing structure, park hopping gets cheaper the longer you stay. With a 3-day ticket, you're paying an extra $19/day per person to hop. That goes down to an extra $7 a day if you're doing an 8-day ticket, and so on.

Taking a look at some of the discount ticket sellers, it appears that a 5-day, non-hopper ticket is going for $348.59. The same 5-day hopper ticket is $362 directly from Disney, which is an extra $19 per ticket.

PARK HOPPING TAKES TIME

I always live by the motto that time is equal to money, especially when on your expensive Disney vacation. Park hopping takes away from the time that you could actually be spending in the parks enjoying the attractions or shows. You have to leave the park, wait for transportation, commute over to the park and then walk to your final destination. This can be hard on your feet, and it can also tire you out faster than just staying in one park.

It may not seem like a lot, but I would rather spend as much time in the parks as possible and not spend it commuting on a Disney bus or walking around. In addition, you'll usually be doing your park hopping in the afternoon. This can put you in the parks right during the busiest times of the day. If you think you're going to hop over to Epcot and ride Soarin' or Test Track in the middle of a busy afternoon period, think again.

YOU DON'T REALLY NEED IT

Park hopping is fun because it allows for flexibility within your schedule, but do you really need it?

When Animal Kingdom was smaller and it only took up half a day to go through the entire park, hopping made more sense. Now, you can easily spend four full days, or more, in each of the parks. So why should we feel the need or pressure to hop?

Save your time and money by enjoying each park from start to finish and from open to close. I love watching each park transform from morning to midday to night time when the lights come on. Something about spending an entire day in a park is especially enjoyable for me.

I found that when my family purchased park hopping tickets, we would always feel the need to take advantage of them because we paid all of that money. Even if we were having a great time in the park or were already getting tired, we would always have to haul ourselves over to another park to make sure we got our money's worth. This takes away from appreciating the experience of a full day in one park. If we wouldn't have had the park hopping option hanging over our heads, we would have stayed put, still had an amazing time and even would have been able to leave with a couple hundred extra dollars in our pockets.

Sometimes grounding yourself in a park allows you to explore those lesser-known attractions, shops or secret areas that you've never experienced before. You could also be like me and ride Rock'n'Roller Coaster and Tower of Terror for two hours straight. (Yes. I did that, and I loved every minute of it.)

For your next trip, I would recommend against purchasing the park hopper option. Pick a different park for each day, and stick with it. Explore the whole park from start to finish instead of trying to race to hit three parks in one day.

There will be many instances where it might make sense to park hop on your trip, which I fully understand. However, if you're able to stick to one park per day, you'll save hundreds of dollars on your vacation. Not only will you save time and money, but also possibly your sanity. Your feet will thank you for it, too!

IS THE "WATER PARKS FUN & MORE" OPTION WORTH IT?

"Water Parks Fun & More" is an option you can choose for your park tickets that will grant you access into additional parks and entertainment options at Disney World.

This will **add an additional $64 per ticket**. The add-on price is the same no matter how many days your base tickets are for. For example, if you choose a 4-day Magic Your Way ticket, you can add a Water Parks & More option for $64. This gives you four entries to select destinations. The add-on price stays consistent regardless of the length of days of your base ticket.

Is it Worth the Price?

This is the main question about this option. **Is it worth the $64 per ticket?** Generally, yes, the option is worth it if you maximize your entries and use them for the water parks.

As mentioned, the $64 is a fixed price per ticket no matter how long your base ticket is for. If you have a 2-day Magic Your Way pass and choose to add Water Parks Fun & More, the two entry options cost $32 each. If you have a 10-day pass, each entry option only costs $6.40 ($64 / 10 = $6). Ten options may seem like a lot, but with each option only costing $6.40, you can still get a lot of value out of most of them while letting the rest expire if you choose to.

In order to see if the add-on is a truly good deal, let's take a look at how much it would cost us if we purchased each of the Water Parks Fun & More options individually:

- **Blizzard Beach:** $56.45 (Ages 10+); $47.93 (Ages 3-9)
- **Typhoon Lagoon:** $56.45 (Ages 10+); $47.93 (Ages 3-9)
- **DisneyQuest** (closing in 2016): $45 (Ages 10+); $39 (Ages 3-9)
- **ESPN Wide World of Sports:** $15.00 (Ages 10+); $10.00 (Ages 3-9)
- **Oak Trail Golf Course:** $38 (per round)

- **Fantasia Gardens Miniature Golf:** $14.00 (Ages 10+); $11.00 (Ages 3-9)
- **Winter Summerland Miniature Golf:** $14.00 (Ages 10+); $11.00 (Ages 3-9)

FRUGAL TIP
BE AWARE THAT THE WATER PARKS WILL CLOSE SOMETIMES DURING THE WINTER DUE TO COLD TEMPERATURES.

As you can see, the prices vary greatly. Depending on the number of entries you get with your Water Parks Fun & More option, you'll probably be getting the best value on the Blizzard Beach and Typhoon Lagoon water parks, followed by Disney Quest and Oak Creek Golf.

Miss tilly sits atop mount mayday overlooking the Wave Pool at Typhoon Lagoon.

The absolute best value you could get from your entries would be to use them for water park visits, but you may get tired of them if you have a lengthy Magic Your Way ticket. From a value perspective, I would not recommend using your options for the mini-golf unless you're just trying to use them up before they expire (or are really into mini-golf!)

If you're planning on visiting **just one water park** during your vacation, it would **be more cost-effective to purchase just a 1-day ticket** to the water park of your choice. If you plan to go to both water parks, or go to a water park and use any of the other options, you will come out ahead by purchasing the Water Parks Fun & More add-on.

If you purchase both the park hopper and Water Parks Fun & More options with your Magic Your Way ticket, you will get a **$34 discount** on both, making it an even better value.

DISNEY FUN FACT
SUMMIT PLUMMET, WHICH IS THE PARK'S ICON SLIDE, MEASURES 120 FEET TALL. YOU CAN REACH SPEEDS OF UP TO 55MPH WHEN GOING DOWN THE SLIDE!

Look at the options you think your family might enjoy, and do the math. Be sure to build some extra days into your vacation to allow you to take full advantage of the options that you'll purchase. If you only have four days and purchase a 4-day Magic Your Way ticket, it probably wouldn't make sense to purchase the Water Parks Fun & More option. You simply won't have enough time.

Here's a tip: At any point in time, you can upgrade a ticket with the Water Parks Fun & More option by going to any ticket booth located at the front gates of the parks. If you're unsure about purchasing that option for some reason, such as the possibility of cool or rainy weather, you can hold off on purchasing it until you arrive.

The Water Parks Fun & More option can be a great way to add additional activities to your Disney vacation at a good value. As long as you effectively utilize the entry options so that the $64 is less than what you would have spent on them individually, you'll be coming out ahead in the end.

The Barry Family's Savings
The Barrys have some tough decisions to make when it comes to purchasing their park tickets. They want the ability to park hop, but need to weigh their options to see if it's worth the cost. They aren't really interested in any of the water parks or add-ons, so those won't need to be purchased.

Using some of the tips in this chapter, Mom Barry calculated how much she could save. At full price, a 4-day park hopper ticket for the whole family comes to a total of $1,678. This will be our starting ticket price.

She decided not to go with the park hopping option. This was a tough choice, but necessary to help save money. Plus, removing that option will allow them to take full advantage of an entire day in each park because they won't feel the need to switch between them. Removing the park hopper option brings the ticket total down to $1,384.

Savings: $294

The next step was to look outside of Disney's prices for some discounted park tickets. While deep discounts don't exist for Disney tickets, some are available through trusted online retailers like Undercover Tourist. As an added bonus, you can get an even bigger discount if you sign up for the Mousesavers newsletter. Currently, a 4-day Magic Your Way ticket is running for $1,376 on Undercover Tourist, which is a slight savings compared to purchasing from Disney themselves.

Savings: $8

This isn't a huge difference, but we've taken their original total of $1,678 down to $1,376. That's a total **savings of $302 on park tickets alone.**

In summary, park tickets will continue to be one of the largest expenses for any Disney vacation. Discounts can be hard to find but, if you follow the strategies and tips outlined in this chapter, you should be able to get yourself a few hundred dollars in savings.

Some of you might have unique requirements for your trip that weren't covered in this section. My advice is to always to run the numbers. Do the math, and find what works best for you.

I'll close out this chapter with a final reminder and word of advice: Never purchase partially-used or "new" tickets from places like Craigslist and Ebay. The prices listed on their sites are very tempting to take advantage of, but resist the urge. You could end up losing all of your money if you purchase from a fraudulent seller.

Always purchase Disney tickets from an official park ticket reseller, from a licensed travel agent or from Disney themselves.

RESORTS AND HOTELS

Now that the Barry family has their flights and park tickets taken care of, it's time to look into places for them to stay during their trip. Hotel options, at first glance, can be overwhelming because of the sheer number of choices. Do you want to stay on-site or off-site? Would you prefer a hotel or a house rental? After you've narrowed it down and chosen the type of place you want to stay, you'll still be presented with many options to choose from.

Hotels prices vary by type: You can find rooms as cheap as $50 a night, or you can spend upwards of $500 per night for a high-end, luxury resort. With literally hundreds of choices in and around Disney property, the competition between hotels helps to keep prices on the lower side.

That doesn't mean, however, that we shouldn't still try our best to reduce or eliminate the costs of hotels for the Barry family's trip, as well as for your own.

The Barry family has looked into two options for their stay: on-site and off-site hotels. Their on-site option is to stay at one of the value resorts. So far, the only resort they've really looked at is Disney's All-Star Sports Resort where a preferred room is currently going for $104/night. This would put their total cost for five nights at just $520. For an off-site option, after using all of the travel search engines, they settled on the Sheraton Lake Buena Vista Resort, which has a rate of $169/night for a total of around $900 total.

Either of these options would already take up a large chunk of their budget. Could there be a better choice? Let's take a look at few strategies and tips that will help them save money on their stay! These will also help you in planning your own family's stay at Disney.

What You Will Learn in this Chapter:
- Off-site vs. on-site - which is a better and cheaper option?
- How to use hotel points for free and discounted nights
- About Disney resort discounts
- Tips to find cheaper hotel rates

*Foosball and a giant Mickey phone in the 70's
section at the Pop Century resort.*

ON-SITE VS. OFF-SITE

The first decision that most people make when choosing a hotel for their stay is if they want to stay on-site, meaning on Disney property, or off-site at one of the neighboring hotels.

When I say "on-site" in this chapter, I'm referring to a Disney owned and operated resort. The Contemporary is an example. Off-site hotels, obviously, are not on Disney property. For simplicity's sake, I will also group all of the on-property but not Disney-owned hotels into the off-site group.

The Barry family really wants to stay on-site during their Disney vacation. On-site Disney resorts offer many benefits:
- Use of the free Magical Express airport shuttle
- Use of Disney transportation
- No need for a rental car
- Access to extra magic hours, which allow you stay in the parks after they close to regular guests
- Being in the "magic" 24/7
- + many other smaller benefits

Staying on-site does come with a few negatives:
- Difficulty getting off-site without a taxi or rental car
- Higher food prices
- Generally smaller room sizes
- Higher room rates
- Being in the "magic" 24/7 (yes this is a negative to some!)

Staying off-site has its benefits as well:
- Flexibility to dine at more varieties of restaurants at cheaper prices
- Easier ability to get to other area attractions such as Universal and SeaWorld
- Easy access to supermarkets
- Cheaper room rates
- Opportunity to cook your own meals
- Ability to use points for free nights

There are some negatives to staying off-site:
- The need to rent a car
- Having to pay for parking when driving to the parks
- Not being in the "magic" 24/7
- Possibility of staying at a low-quality hotel

While I can't make the actual decision of staying on-site or off-site for you, you can use these lists of pros and cons to decide what is best for your family. I'll provide a few additional, helpful tips below as well.

Staying on-site gives you access to Disney's Magical Express service.

When I make decisions like this, I start by looking at the deal breakers. For example, if you really don't want to have to rent a car or drive while you're there, that would definitely sway you toward choosing to stay on-site. However, if you plan to visit Universal or SeaWorld or take a trip out to Cape Canaveral, you may want to think about staying off-site.

FRUGAL TIP

IF YOU PLAN TO STAY OFF-SITE, BE SURE TO THOROUGHLY CHECK SITES LIKE TRIP ADVISOR (WWW.TRIPADVISOR.COM) TO SEE REAL PICTURES AND ACTUAL GUEST REVIEWS.

I will say that, strictly from a money-saving perspective, you have more opportunities to save when you stay off-site. Throughout this chapter, you'll see that you can only hit a certain percentage of savings when staying on-site. The opportunity to save higher amounts of money comes with staying outside Disney property.

Personally, I have stayed both on and off-site during my many, many trips and have always enjoyed myself no matter which location I chose. I'm confident that whichever you choose, you'll have an amazing time!

USING HOTEL POINTS FOR FREE & DISCOUNTED NIGHTS

One of the best options to help reduce, and even completely remove, the cost of hotel stays is to use free hotel points obtained through credit card sign-up bonuses. (See? These sign-up bonuses can help you save money on flights AND on hotels.) In this section, I'm going to show you how you can stay for free at certain hotels and how you can cut costs of your stay at others by over 50 percent. In particular, I'll show you how you can stay for free at one of the best resorts on Disney property: The Swan and Dolphin.

When I started breaking down costs of my own Disney vacations, one item always stood out as being one of the most costly: hotels. Even if you stay at a lower-cost hotel with room rates around $75/night, your total for a five-night stay is almost $500 after taxes and fees.

After realizing this, I got to work by first looking into ways to save as much money as possible on hotels. Then, I went even further by searching for ways to stay for free. After doing quite a bit of research, I discovered several ways to stay for free, or for pennies on the dollar, at some of the best hotels in the world.

Using the methods outlined in this chapter, I've stayed at hotels in Disney World, Paris, Belgium, Rome, Venice, Seattle and many more - all for free or for pennies on the dollar! I also want to point out that I'm not talking about hostels or Motel 8's here. I'm talking about top-level, name brand hotel chains like Hiltons, Sheratons, Radissons, Intercontinentals and more.

HOW TO GET FREE NIGHTS

How are you going to get hotels to give you free nights when they could be charging hundreds of dollars per night? All major hotel chains have loyalty programs to entice frequent travelers to continue to stay at their hotels.

Hotels award their frequent customers with points that are based on how much money they spend on rooms at that hotel. Let's take Hilton's loyalty program, HHonors, for example. It awards members 10 points for every dollar spent on their hotel room. If you spend $800 on a stay at a Hilton hotel, you would be awarded 8,000 HHonors points that can then be redeemed for free nights.

If you're like me, the amount you spend on hotels hardly gives you enough points to redeem for free nights. Luckily for us, that's not a problem at all. There are ways to get thousands of hotel points without ever setting foot in a hotel.

Each major hotel brand has their own set of branded credit cards that are issued by major banks: American Express, Chase, Citi and Bank of America, among others. To encourage people to sign up for these credit cards, the banks offer sign-up bonuses in the form of hotel points usually awarded after you meet a spendings requirement on the card.

The main way to get a lot of redeemable points is by signing up for these credit cards and meeting the spendings requirements.

Let's take a look at how to stay at a Starwood brand hotel for a short trip down to Disney. A few of Starwood's brands include Sheraton, Westin, Aloft, W, Four Points, and the Swan and Dolphin. The Swan and Dolphin Resort includes two separate hotels: The Swan and The Dolphin. Both are technically Westins, and we are going to focus on them for most of this chapter.

The beautiful Swan/Dolphin Resort

Starwood's loyalty program is called Starwood Preferred Guest (SPG), and it is by far my favorite hotel loyalty program. SPG's currency is Starpoints, which are very valuable to redeem for free nights. Since the Swan and Dolphin are Westins, both fall under Starwood's SPG program and allow you to redeem your Starpoints for free nights.

As we search for ways to help the hypothetical Barrys get great deals on hotels for their trip in May, I'll show you step by step how to do the same for your own vacation.

LET'S GET SOME HOTEL POINTS

Before you start earning your points, you'll want to go apply for a free SPG account. This is where you'll store your Starpoints after you earn them.

1. Go to SPG.com and create an account so you have a place to store your Starpoints.

2. Click "Join now," complete the registration process and take note of your SPG number. I recommend using Awardwallet.com to track all of your loyalty program accounts.

Before you move forward, make sure that you have your credit in order and that it is above 700 like I mentioned in the Travel to Disney chapter. You'll need to have good enough credit to be able to get the credit cards, which will give us free hotel nights.

After doing the groundwork, you'll then apply for the SPG card from American Express. This is one of my favorite credit cards to have. It will give you **25,000 Starpoints** after you spend **$5,000 in six months.** You'll also receive an additional point for each dollar spent. So, including the sign-up spendings, you'll have 30,000 Starpoints. Be sure to include your SPG number in your application. If you don't already have one, one will be assigned to you.

DISNEY FUN FACT
DISNEY HAS OVER 27,000 HOTEL ROOMS ON PROPERTY AND CONTINUES TO GROW THAT NUMBER.

Spending $5,000 might seem like a lot, but that's only about $840 per month for six months. This can easily be done if you put all of your spendings on the card. Just be sure to pay it off at the end of each month!

After you've hit your spendings amount, you should have at least 30,000 Starpoints in your account. This definitely will be enough to get you some free nights at the Swan and Dolphin Resort!

HOW TO BOOK YOUR FREE NIGHTS

Now it's time for the fun part: using the points you earned to get some free nights!

In addition to the Swan and Dolphin, Starwood has a number of properties in the Lake Buena Vista area. There are six within a close proximity to Disney World, so you could also look into booking those with your points.

Each Starwood hotel has a category associated with it that determines room rates, award redemption rates and amenities. Categories range from 1-8, with 1 being the least expensive and 8 being super-luxury hotels.

Here is a chart of the closest Starwood hotels to Disney and their category ratings, points required per free night and Tripadvisor ratings.

Hotel	Category	Free Night Points	Points + Cash	Tripadvisor Rating
Walt Disney World Swan	4	10,000	5000 + $75	75%
Walt Disney World Dolphin	4	10,000	5000 + $75	75%
Sheraton Lake Buena Vista	3	7,000	3500 + $55	69%
Sheraton Vistana Resort Villas	4	10,000	5000 + $75	82%
Sheraton Vistana Villiages I-Drive	4	10,000	5000 + $75	83%
Westin Orlando Universal Blvd	4	10,000	5000 + $75	85%

Looking at the chart above, you'll need to redeem either 10,000 points or 5,000 points + $75 for a free night at the Swan and Dolphin.

The enormous pool at the Sheraton Vistana Villiages

Head on over to http://www.SPG.com where you can search for available hotels during the desired dates of your next vacation. If you aren't sure when it will be yet, you can use the dates of the Barry family's vacation: May 15 - May 19.

In the destination box, enter "Lake Buena Vista" as the city. Click "Find Now" to get the results and availability for those dates. You'll see a list of available hotels during that date range. From this screen, you can click through and read all of the details for each hotel.

spg. Starwood Preferred Guest	Q BOOK & REDEEM ˅	≡ ABOUT SPG ˅	⩗ SIGN IN ˅	USER
CLICK RATE NAME TO CHANGE	Lowest Standard Rate ✎	SPG Free Nights ✎	SPG Cash & Points ✎	
Sheraton Lake Buena Vista Resort	From **USD $143** per night ›	From **3,000 Starpoints** per night ›	Find Available Dates ›	
Walt Disney World Swan	From **USD $196** per night ›	From **10,000 Starpoints** per night ›	From **5,000 Starpoints** +USD $75 per night ›	
Walt Disney World Dolphin	From **USD $214** per night ›	From **10,000 Starpoints** per night ›	From **5,000 Starpoints** +USD $75 per night ›	

I like to use the compare rates screen, which allows you to see some of the other hotel rate options available to choose from, such as the standard rates, cash and points option, plus a few other rates you could book as well.

FRUGAL TIP

ALL MAJOR HOTEL CHAINS HAVE LOYALTY PROGRAMS AND BRANDED CREDIT CARDS. BE SURE TO CHECK OUT HILTON, MARRIOTT AND IHG FOR GOOD HOTEL OPTIONS.

As you can see, you have many options when it comes to paying for your room. Some of the higher-end properties cost from 7,000 -10,000 Starpoints per night.

With 30,000 Starpoints from your SPG card, you could redeem them for **three free nights at the Dolphin!**

WHY I LOVE CASH AND POINTS

I want to take a moment to talk about one of the best uses of SPG points: cash and points rewards. Just as the name states, cash and points allow you to split the cost of a room between Starpoints and cash. For example, a category 4 like the Swan and Dolphin would be 10,000 points for a free night or 5,000 points and $75/night.

While not free, $75 a night for the Swan and Dolphin is a spectacular deal! You're also getting great value out of your Starpoints at 2.2 cents a piece. (Math: $210/night - $75/ night = $135/5000 points = 0.0278 or 2.8 cents per point.)

If you want to use points exclusively, I would choose the Sheraton Lake Buena Vista Resort at a cost of 28,000 points, which will give you **four free nights.**

The Swan and Dolphin is an excellent resort, and it has the additional perk of being on-site. You can't beat the location: It's nestled right between Hollywood Studios and Epcot. Plus, you get extra perks like being able to take advantage of extra magic hours.

Mom Barry is very tempted to choose the Dolphin for their vacation. However, they only have enough points for three nights. Is it possible to get enough points for four free nights? Let's see.

How to Use Free Nights + Cash & Points

You can combine reward booking options by redeeming some SPG points for free nights and some for cash and points. This flexibility allows you to minimize your out-of-pocket costs and stretch your points a little further.

In the case of the Barry family, they could do the following with their 30,000 Starpoints:
* Book two free award nights for a total of 20,000 points.
* Book the second two nights using cash and points award nights, for a cost of 10,000 points and $150.

If they went that route, they would use up all 30,000 points and only pay $150 + $64 (fees) in cash. That comes out to **$37.50/night**, which is not bad for the Dolphin!

If they were to book a full price room, it would be $189/night, for a grand total (including fees) of $980. They would have **a savings of $830!**

I'll go over the Barry family's final decision at the end of this chapter.

To officially book your room, you'll just complete the process through the website or call SPG at 1-888-625-4988. I highly recommend booking hotel award nights as early as possible because you can always cancel and adjust dates if you need to, without any penalties. Remember to always double-check the fine print.

The ability to stay on-site at the Swan and Dolphin and use cash and point awards are just a few of the reasons that I love using Starpoints for my Disney stays. Many other options exist from other hotel chains such as Hilton, IHG, and Club Carlson. I hope this section saves your family hundreds, and maybe thousands of dollars on your next vacation.

DISNEY RESORT DISCOUNTS

Disney regularly releases discounts for their resorts from 15 percent up to 30 percent. The two main types you'll see are room-only discounts and package discounts.

Room-only discounts are exactly as they sound: just for the room itself with no tickets or transportation included. The package discounts bundle together the room and tickets, and sometimes a dining package, for an overall discount on your stay. For simplicity's sake, we'll just group these together and call them Disney resort discounts. When you're booking, be sure to check what the discount actually entails.

Disney offers discounts on their resorts in a few ways:

- **Publicly Available Offers:** You'll find these offers on the Disney website, as well as sites like frugalmouse.com that post them as soon as they are available. Anyone can book these discount rates through a travel agent or on the web.

- **Pin Code Offers:** Disney will sometimes target certain people with special offers such as room discounts or dining promotions. Each family gets their own unique pin code that can be used for discounts.

- **Bounce Back Offers:** These are offered to guests who are currently at the end of their Disney vacation. You might get a call or a special offer during checkout for a discount on a future trip. The only catch is that you have to book it before you leave.

Disney usually releases resort discounts one full season prior to the season that the discount is being offered for. For example, if Disney were to release a 30 percent room-only discount offer for the fall, you'll see that offer released one season early - during the summer.

Can't beat a monorail going through the middle of your resort.

When booking a Disney-offered resort promotion, here are some tips to help you get the most out of it:

- The number of rooms allocated for promotions at each resort are limited. If you are looking to take advantage of a promotion, make sure to book early before the discounted rooms run out.

- You can apply a newly-released discount on a previous booking. If you already have a room booked but hear about a newly released offer, you can call up Disney and have the promotion applied to your room.

- Disney can split discounts if some of your dates fall outside of the promotional period. For example, if the first three nights of your stay fall within dates that are part of a promotion but the last two are not, you can get the discount on just those three nights.

Disney does structure their discounts interestingly, which could be a bad thing for those of us who are booking the "cheaper" rooms. When you hear about their promotions, you'll always hear phrases such as "up to 30 percent off." The words "up to" are key. The cheaper the room rates are, the lower the discount will be.

Value resorts usually see a 10 -15 percent discount, moderates 15 - 25 percent and the deluxe resorts 25 - 30 percent. You have to spend more money to save more money which, in some cases, may be worth it. You will have to do the math to see what works best for you and your family.

Here are a few last tips that you can use to save money staying at a Disney Resort:

- **Stay at the value resorts:** I've experienced all categories of the resorts on property from the value to the deluxe. I don't find the premium cost of the higher end resorts worth it when you're spending most of your time at the parks. The value resorts are clean, have large pools and are easy on the wallet!

- **Do you really need a view?** I always recommend paying for the lowest "garden" view rooms which will save you money. I rarely find the views all that great to begin with at Disney resorts, and you'll be paying a premium for something you don't need.

RENTING DISNEY VACATION CLUB POINTS

The Disney Vacation Club, or DVC for short, is Disney's version of a vacation ownership club. This is also known as a timeshare. With a timeshare, you are basically pre-paying (a lot of money) up front for your vacations over the course of a certain number of years you choose. In just about all cases, buying into a timeshare is not going to save you money and will usually end up costing more than just staying at hotels/resorts using standard rates.

You will see DVC salespeople and kiosks all over the place on your trip to Disney, and they will try hard to sell to you by making it seem like an amazing deal. Trust me when I say that it's far from a good deal. In fact, in just about all cases, it's a very bad deal.

The Bay Lake Tower, which is connected to the Contemporary Resort, is a Disney Vacation Club Resort.

DVC has a fairly unique system for ownership in the form of a points system. When you sign up for the club, you purchase a set number of points each year with a minimum purchase of 100 points per year. You have to sign a contract stating the number of years that you'll be part of the program. Each point costs $140-$160, depending on which resort you choose as your home resort. At a minimum, you'll be paying a whopping $14,000 per year just to be part of the DVC, which is a huge sum of money.

So why am I even mentioning the DVC at its obscene price?

Because we can take advantage of the DVC by renting points from their members for as little as $12/point to stay at the luxurious resorts that are part of the DVC.

When a DVC member isn't able to use up all of their points in a given year, they have the ability to "rent" them out to others who can then use those points to stay at the DVC resorts. Renting DVC points generally costs between $12-$17 a point, which is a huge discount off of what the member paid. This can save you hundreds or even thousands of dollars on a resort stay when compared to paying the "rack" or standard rates.

Here's an example

Let's say you would like to stay at the Boardwalk Inn resort's villas for five nights in October. You'll have to find the number of points needed for this stay. Simply search Google for "DVC Point Charts," and you'll find many sites with the charts. Find the Boardwalk Inn villas and the dates of your intended stay to see the number of points needed per night.

Looking at the Boardwalk Inn resort's point prices, a stay in a studio room that sleeps four would require 10 points/night for a total of 50 points. A DVC member could rent 50 points to you at $13/point for a grand total of $650 or $130/night.

If you were to book from Disneyworld.com, the same room runs an average of $469/night for a total of $2,345!

You potentially would be saving a whopping $1,695 ($2,354 - $650) by renting DVC points instead of booking a standard rack-rate room. Even if you had to pay much more than $13/point, you would still be coming out way ahead.

A big positive about DVC resorts is the ability to stay in their villas, which are available as one and two bedrooms and also have kitchens. This allows much larger families or groups to be accommodated plus the potential money savings of being able to cook meals in the villa.

Next, you'll need to get in contact with a DVC member that is willing to rent you their points for a low price. You can do this a couple of ways:

- Go through a DVC rental forum such as http://www.mouseowners.com/, which is one of my favorite DVC sites that connects owners with renters. It has forums dedicated to connecting DVC members with renters. This will be the cheapest method, and it will give you some room to bargain down the price of a point.

- Go through a DVC rental site such as https://www.dvcrequest.com/, which handles the transactions of renting points for you. With this method, they will act as the go-between and handle all of the needed transactions. You will pay an extra $2-$3 extra per point for their services but you have the added protection of their guarantees.

If you choose to connect directly with a DVC member, here is how the process works:

1. Choose a resort or several resorts that you would like to stay at, along with dates that you're looking to stay. Using a points chart, find how many points you'll need for that stay. You can probably assume an average of $13/point in general, so do the math to see how much that will cost you.

2. Go to the DVC rental forums site and post the dates and resort(s) you're looking for. For example, if you're looking to stay at the Boardwalk Villas from 10/4 to 10/10, you would just post that as the request.

3. If a DVC member has points available, they will respond to your post with an offer for your requested dates and resort(s).You'll probably see a variation in point values, anywhere from $12-$17 per point. You are allowed to negotiate, so feel free to make a counteroffer to see if they'll accept.

4. When you agree on the price for the points, the DVC member will have to make the reservation for you under your name and information. This is very important: When it comes time for payment, be sure ONLY to use PayPal as a payment method, as it provides you with purchaser protection.

A few words of caution when using this method to book rooms.

1. You will have to send money to the DVC member who will be booking the rooms for you under you name. This presents a bit of risk, as technically that person could run off with your money. This brings me to point #2.

2. Only pay the DVC member using PayPal, which has purchaser protections. If for some unlikely reason you run into an issue, you would be protected and receive a refund from PayPal.

3. Any changes/modifications to the room would have to be done by the DVC member, which can be a bit of a hassle.

If you are worried about any of these scenarios, I suggest you go through a DVC booking site which will prevent these issues but cost you a bit more.

This method of renting DVC points potentially can save you hundreds or even thousands of dollars when comparing prices with the standard rates. Depending on the resort and the time of year you choose to go, it can still be on the expensive side. So make sure to check the point requirements!

FINDING OFF-SITE ROOM AND HOUSE DISCOUNTS

The number of hotels that are within a few miles of Disney property is probably in the hundreds. That's a lot of competition out there between hotels to attract customers.

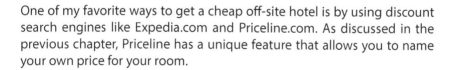

FRUGAL TIP

ALWAYS TRY TO BARGAIN DOWN THE PRICE PER NIGHT WITH THE HOUSE OWNERS. NINE TIMES OUT OF 10, THEY WILL LOWER THE RATE FOR YOU. ALL YOU NEED TO DO IS ASK.

One of my favorite ways to get a cheap off-site hotel is by using discount search engines like Expedia.com and Priceline.com. As discussed in the previous chapter, Priceline has a unique feature that allows you to name your own price for your room.

When using Priceline to bid for a room, you'll first want to see what the current rates are for your desired type of hotel (1-5 star) and general location area.

After you have an idea of the going rates for the hotels in the area, you should start bidding at a 25 percent discount and slowly work your way up. You might get lucky and score a room right away at a 25 percent discount, or you might need to lower the discount rate a bit.

Another option that many families take advantage of is renting a house for their vacation stays. This can be an excellent option to consider, as houses can be the same price or sometimes cheaper per night than a hotel. With a house, you get a ton of space, a full kitchen and parking. Many also have their own private pools.

Houses are an especially good option for larger families or groups. With a house, everyone can stay in the same location and save a lot of money instead of having to stay in multiple hotel rooms.

Check out sites like homeaway.com, airbnb.com and VBRO.com to find listings of rental houses near Disney.

THE BARRY FAMILY'S CHOICE OF STAY AT DISNEY

The Barry family has many options to consider when it comes to their hotel stay at Disney. They want to stay at an on-site hotel, and they may have found the perfect way to do that and save money at the same time.

That perfect combination is the example we discussed earlier: using Starpoints for free nights at the Swan and Dolphin. While the Swan and Dolphin are operated by Starwood hotels, they are right in the Epcot resort area. Guests staying there have access to Disney transportation and extra magic hours.

The one downside is that they will not have access to the Magical Express service, so they will need to arrange transportation or rent a car, which adds some cost.

The Barry family will be staying for five nights from May 15 through May 19, so the cash amount for their stay at the Swan would be a total of $1,145 ($219/night x 5). Mom Barry got 30,000 Starpoints after signing up for the SPG credit card and fulfilling the spendings amount, which will be enough to cover their stay using the cash + points option.

For each night, the cash + points rate is 5,000 points + $75. For five nights, that comes to a total of 25,000 points + $375.

Only paying $375 out of pocket, compared with a full cash rate of $1,145, represents a **total savings of $770!**

The Swan and Dolphin is one of the best resorts in the Disney area, so getting five nights at only $375 in total is a huge savings for the Barry family.

If you don't choose to go the hotel points route, you can still stay in an affordable on-site or off-site resort. To summarize this chapter, the best way to save money on hotels and resorts are as follows:

- Use hotel points to get free or discounted nights.
- Stay at an off-site resort or house.
- Use travel search engines like Expedia, Priceline or Orbitz to search for cheaper rates.
- Travel during off-peak times when room rates are cheaper.
- Keep an eye out for Disney resort discounts one season prior to your trip.

FOOD

Food and drink will always be another major expense for anyone going on a Disney vacation. Disney knows they've got you. Let's face it: When you're in the parks and start to get hungry, those $4.50 pretzels suddenly seem to be worth every penny.

The problem with food costs is that they add up quickly. Park food is usually right at that price point where it may not seem like you're spending much at the time. Spending $9 to $12 for a meal at most quick-service locations probably isn't that bad in the grand scheme of things. However, multiply that by a few days and a few people, and it quickly adds up. (The amount they charge for the quality of park food provided is another topic entirely. Maybe I'll save that one for another book.)

Before we get into the meat of this chapter, I must admit that I love food. Disney has a wide selection of food in their parks and resorts. Whenever I'm traveling, food is always a major part of my excitement of getting there. It's no different when I go to Disney World.

If you're working on planning your first trip to Disney, I highly recommend you pick at least one nice meal to enjoy while you're there. Let's not forget you're on vacation! At least once during each trip, I'll usually splurge a bit on a nice, sit-down meal at one of the countries at Epcot or at a resort.

All of the strategies outlined in this chapter will help you offset the cost of your meal splurge and save some money overall.

What You Will Learn in this Chapter:

- A breakdown of a typical food costs
- How to redeem points for free restaurant gift cards
- Tips for saving money on breakfast
- How to get free water
- How to save money by dining off-site
- All about free dining packages

JUST HOW EXPENSIVE IS FOOD?

To illustrate how quickly food costs can add up, let's do some math for the Barry family's vacation.

We already know that their family will be staying at the Swan and Dolphin resort in May for five days and five nights. We also know that they decided to purchase 4-day Magic Your Way passes for the Disney parks.

The Barrys opted not to go with a Disney Dining plan because, unless you happen to catch a promotion, those can be very expensive. They felt that they could save money by planning their own meals. I recommend that you do the same for your vacation.

Those Mickey Waffles are delicious, but pricey.

I don't want to bore you with planning out meals for each day, so we'll use this day at the Magic Kingdom shown below to give us an average spendings on food per day in the parks for the Barry family.

DAY 1
Breakfast at the food court
Mom - Veggie Omelette: $7.69
Dad - Western Omelette: $7.99
Bobby - Mickey Waffle: $6.39
Susy - Mickey Waffle: $4.99 (kids)

4 x Water: $11
Breakfast Total: $38.06

Lunch at Cosmic Ray's Starlight Cafe
Mom - Grilled Chicken Sandwich: $10.79
Dad - 1/2 Rotisserie Chicken: $10.99
Bobby - Hot Dog: $8.29
Susy - Chicken Nuggets: $5.99 (kids)
4 x Water: $11
Lunch Total: $47.06

Dinner at Columbia Harbor House
Mom - Anchors Aweigh Sandwich: $9.49
Dad - Battered Fish Sandwich: $8.49
Bobby - Chicken Nuggets: $8.99
Susy - Macaroni & Cheese: $5.99 (kids)
4 x Water: $11
Dinner Total: $43.96

Snacks
Mom - Dole Whip: $5.29
Dad - Dole Whip: $5.29
Bobby - Ice cream: $3.69
Susy - Chocolate Chip cookie: $2.59 (kids)
4 x Water: $11
Snacks Total: $27.86

You can see that the average meal comes out to $43.03. This includes some snacks and water that will be needed throughout the day because I don't think anyone can walk by the Dole Whip stand and not have one. Their grand total for food is a whopping **$156.94**. If we multiply that by the four days that they'll be at the parks, their grand total for food on this trip will be **$627.76!**

Surprisingly, that is even on the low side of what you could spend. The example day above didn't include going to Epcot for some drinks around the world, which go for $9 - $13 each. It also didn't account for that nice sit-down meal I suggest every family does at least once. Taking those things into account, realistically, the Barrys could easily spend around $700 - $1,000 for this relatively quick trip. The same applies to your family! This is actually close to the amount they spent on food during their last vacation. Let's see if we can get that down for their next one!

DISNEY FUN FACT
OVER 7,000,000 CHEESEBURGERS ARE SERVED IN THE PARKS EACH YEAR!

Food prices at Disney World are high because people will pay them. Unless you pack your breakfast, lunch, dinner and snacks, which isn't exactly practical, you're going to spend some money on meals during your vacation. I, for one, am not looking to eat peanut butter and jelly sandwiches for lunch and dinner when I'm on vacation, even though it'll save a lot of money. Dining out and trying new foods is an important part of the overall vacation experience for many families. I do not recommend cutting it out completely!

With that said, I looked into and successfully found ways to manage the costs of eating at Disney: shortcuts, tips and ideas that can help take the sting out of the high food prices. So, now that we have this baseline food price of $700 for a family of four taking a 4- to 5-day trip to Disney, let's look at some of these practical ways both you and the Barry family can save money.

REDEEMING CREDIT CARD POINTS FOR RESTAURANT GIFT CARDS

Not only are credit card points from Chase (Ultimate Rewards), American Express (Membership Rewards) and Citi (Thank You Points) great for getting lower prices on hotels and flights, but they are also redeemable for gift cards. While I tend to discourage redeeming valuable points for gift cards, this can be an option if you have some extra points to help save money on food.

I'm generally not a huge fan of redeeming those points for gift cards because, at most, you'll get a penny per point. That means if you have 20,000 Citi Thank You points in your account, you can redeem those for a $200 gift card to a restaurant.

A $100 gift card to Darden Restaurants (Olive Garden, Longhorn Steakhouse, Red Lobster) will cost you 10,000 Chase Ultimate Rewards points.

Of course, you'll have to venture off property to redeem these gift cards but, hey, it could potentially mean a highly discounted or even free dinner. Some off-site restaurants that you can get gift cards for are:

- Olive Garden
- Applebees
- Chili's
- Longhorn Steakhouse
- Red Lobster
- Outback Steakhouse
- + many others

Perhaps the best value when redeeming Thank You points is for a Landry's restaurants gift card. Landry's has a large range of restaurants, including even a few restaurants on-site:

- Yak & Yeti Restaurant in Animal Kingdom (both sit down and counter service)
- Rainforest Cafe in Animal Kingdom and Downtown Disney (Disney Springs)
- T-Rex Restaurant in Downtown Disney (Disney Springs)

I've confirmed with all locations at Disney that they accept the Landry's gift cards.

How do you go about getting points that you can use to get hundreds of dollars of free gift cards?

Step 1

Apply for a credit card that earns Chase Ultimate Rewards, Citi Thank You or American Express Membership Rewards points. The process is the same for all cards, but we'll use Citi Thank You points for this example.

My card of choice at the moment is the Citi Premier Thank You Card, which will give you 50,000 Thank You points after spending $3,000 in the first three months of having the card. That's only $1,000/month, which shouldn't be too hard to hit if you charge everything to your credit card.

You'll also earn one extra point for each of those $3,000 you spend. After hitting the spendings requirement, you will have, at a minimum, 53,000 Thank You points. These can be redeemed for $530 in gift cards to restaurants. It shouldn't cost you anything extra to get those gift cards, so you'll be **cutting your food bill by over $530**. That's great savings!

Step 2

After hitting the spendings requirement and being awarded your Thank You points, you can log in to the Thank You rewards site to begin shopping for your gift cards. My favorite redemption, as I mentioned, is the Landry's restaurants gift card because of the dining options on-site, such as the Yak & Yeti in Animal Kingdom, plus many options off-site as well.

Step 3

Choose the denomination of gift card that you would like to redeem your points for. They only come as high as $100 a card, so I would choose five $100 gift cards and one $25 gift card for a total of 52,500 Thank You points

Landry's Gift Card

Starting at
2,500 points

Please make a selection below

| Denomination: | $25 | $50 | $100 |

Quantity: ∞ 1 +

Delivery Type: ? Mail

🛒 ADD TO CART   ♥

Step 4

Go through the checkout process, and your gift cards will be on their way! When they do arrive, be sure to keep them in a safe place. They're as good as cash.

The great thing about getting these gift cards is that Landry's has restaurant locations all over the country. So, if you only use up $300 of them while on vacation, there's likely to be a restaurant close to where you live. You can use them at home, too!

It can be so difficult to find ways to save money on food while on vacation. I've been there! Being able to save over $500 on food with just a single credit card application can really help keep costs down on your next Disney trip. Most of the restaurants that you can get gift cards for are off-site but, as mentioned, Landry's offer a unique benefit of being able to use them on-site for restaurants as well.

Since the Barry family loves the Yak & Yeti restaurant, they decided to take advantage of this gift card strategy and get a free dinner for one night of their trip! They redeemed 15,000 points for a $150 gift card to Landry's restaurants, which will give them a **completely free meal at Yak & Yeti.**

CHARACTER DINING ON THE CHEAP

One of the most popular meals at the parks, which can fill up months in advance, is character dining. It's a favorite among kids, and having the characters come up to have fun while you're enjoying a meal builds memories that will last a lifetime. Character dining meals are available for breakfast, lunch and dinner at various restaurants. Some of the most popular character dining restaurants are:

- Chef Mickey's at the Contemporary Resort

- Cinderella's Royal Table at Magic Kingdom

- Crystal Palace at Magic Kingdom

- 1900 Park Fare and the Grand Floridian

The problem with character dining is the very high cost of the meals. Most are buffets, so you can try to eat your money's worth, but you'll still be paying between $19 - $29 for kids and $29 - $60+ for adults. The price variations are due to the different costs of restaurants, as well as seasonally adjusted pricing.

Breakfast is always cheaper than lunch, and lunch is always cheaper than dinner. If you must choose one meal to do character dining, breakfast will be your cheapest option.

Say, for example, the Barry family wanted to go to Chef Mickey's character dining for breakfast one morning of their trip. The cost of the buffet is $19/kids, $38/adult + tip, which would come to a whopping total of $137! Just for breakfast!

There's no way they are going to be spending $137 for breakfast, so I'll let you in on a secret that many people don't know about - The Garden Grove restaurant at the Swan Resort.

It's not the most well-known restaurant, and even less known is the fact that it features character dining for breakfast on the weekends and for dinner nightly. Prices are much more reasonable for their breakfast buffet - $16 for children 3-9 and $25 for adults. This is much cheaper than any of the other character dining options.

The dinner menu has a few options and an unlimited soup/salad bar and dessert bar. Prices range from $18 for children ages 3-9 and $29-$36 for adults, depending on which entree you choose. While all of these prices aren't necessarily inexpensive, this is your most frugal option if you are looking to do a character meal.

If the Barry family chose to go with this character dining option, it would cost them a total of $98, which is much cheaper than Chef Mickey's. While $98 is still a steep price to pay for breakfast, it may be worth the splurge to see your family having a great time dining with the characters!

EATING BREAKFAST AND SNACKS IN YOUR HOTEL ROOM

By far, the easiest meal of the day to save money on is the first one - breakfast. I don't mean that you should save money by skipping breakfast entirely. We all know that's not a good thing to do. Some actually say it's the most important meal of the day! On my trips to Disney, I rarely eat breakfast at the resort or in the parks. It's just too expensive, and it's actually very easy to avoid that extra cost.

Just about all hotel rooms have a coffee maker, a fridge and a microwave. This gives you the opportunity to cook many things for breakfast right in your hotel room, and it will definitely save you money on meals each day.

In addition to saving money, eating breakfast in your room helps you get an earlier jump on the day. I'm a huge proponent of getting to the parks right when they open. That way, you can hit the big attractions first and won't wind up stuck in long lines for them all day. I'd rather eat a quick and cheap breakfast in my hotel room and get to the parks early than spend extra time and money going to breakfast at a restaurant.

Travelers to Disney fall into two categories: those with a car and those without. If you do have a car, this can make it easier to take a trip to the grocery store to pick up breakfast items to keep in your room.

If you're staying on-site or won't have access to a car, you're not out of luck. You can pack breakfast foods and snacks in your luggage to bring along with you. Just be aware that the TSA might categorize some items in your carry-on luggage as liquids, so you might want to check food unless it's a solid item.

A few items that I usually bring along or pick up at a supermarket are:
- Bagels and cream cheese or peanut butter
- Instant oatmeal
- Granola bars
- Chips/pretzels
- Cereal
- Fruit
- Yogurt
- Breakfast pastries

If you really want to get adventurous, and if there is a microwave in your hotel room, you could even cook things like bacon and eggs for a full breakfast in your hotel room.

Here is how to cook bacon and eggs in a microwave:
1. Place two sheets of paper towel on a microwave-safe plate.
2. Lay up to 8 slices of bacon on the paper towels. Make sure you don't overlap the slices.
3. Place two more sheets of paper towel on top.

4. Heat in the microwave on high for 4 to 6 minutes.
5. Scramble eggs in a microwave-safe bowl or cup (coffee mugs work well).
6. Microwave for 45 seconds, remove and stir.
7. Microwave for 30 seconds.

Now you have a full bacon and eggs breakfast that was made in less than 10 minutes in your hotel room. This would cost you at least $10 at the resort food court. Your actual cost? Less than $2 per serving.

Eating breakfast in your hotel room may not seem that enjoyable, but it will really help you with money savings over the course of a trip. Let's use the Barry family of four again to illustrate this. If they choose to eat breakfast out somewhere each of their five days, they could easily spend at least $8/person per day. That adds up to $160+ for the course of the trip.

Mom Barry read this tip on Frugal Mouse months ago, which allowed her to plan ahead to eat breakfast in the hotel room. To save money on breakfast during their trip, she is going to pack bagels, oatmeal, granola bars and fruit that the family could eat before heading to the parks.

Cosmic Ray's Starlight Cafe in the Magic Kingdom
has a good variety of food options.

All of this food will only cost her $25, and she will pack it in everyone's carry-on luggage for the trip down from Philadelphia. For the cost of less than one breakfast at the food court, mom will be able to feed her family breakfast for all five days of the trip.

It's amazing to think that, originally, they were planning to spend around $38/day for breakfast at the food court, for a total of $160+ for the whole duration of their stay at Disney! We've now cut that cost down to $25!

PLANNING YOUR MEALS STRATEGICALLY

I always love sitting down for a meal at the parks, especially when going to Epcot to sample the varieties of food from around the world. Sitting down for a meal helps break up your day and gives you some time to rest, relax and refuel.

I would normally be eating at a quick-service restaurant for my meals but, hey, we're on vacation. Why not treat ourselves to at least one nice, full-service meal? Sitting down for a full-service meal doesn't mean we need to break our food budgets.

When I do choose to do a sit-down meal at a full-service restaurant, it is always for a late lunch. Why?

Restaurants Are Less Crowded

Many people wait to sit down for dinner, which often leaves plenty of seating availability during lunch. Many times, even during peak periods, I've been able to walk up to a sit-down restaurant and get in with little or no wait. If you do have a specific time or place in mind to eat, I would recommend getting a reservation ahead of time. Just in case! After you're done eating, you could go back and hit some of the most popular attractions because people will be in restaurants eating dinner instead of on the rides and at shows.

FRUGAL TIP

ALWAYS CHECK AT THE FRONT DESK OF RESTAURANTS, EVEN IF THEY ARE SHOWING AS FULL. MOST TIMES, THERE ARE CANCELLATIONS OR NO-SHOWS, WHICH CAN GET YOU IN QUICKLY!

It's Cheaper

At some restaurants, Disney prices their lunch dishes slightly lower than dinner dishes. Lunch menus are generally 15 - 20 percent cheaper, even though many of those restaurants serve the exact same menu items for dinner.

For example, the San Angel Inn and Chef Mickey's both have different prices for their lunch entrees and their dinner entrees. I took the average of the lunch entrees vs. the dinner entrees and compared them on the table below.

Restaurant	Avg Lunch Entree Price	Avg Dinner Entree Price	Difference ($/%)
San Angel Inn	$21.84	$26.83	$4.99 / 18.5%
Chef Mickey's	$40.46 (buffet price)	$50.05 (buffet price)	$9.59 / 19%

As you can see, you'll save a bit of money if you dine at these restaurants during lunch instead of dinner. Some of the entrees do change from lunch to dinner, but you'll still get the same amount and the same quality of food at lunch. You'll just pay a slight premium for dining during the dinner hours.

The Mexico pavilion at Epcot with the tasty San Angel Inn restaurant inside.

It is important to note that not all restaurants have variable pricing like this for lunch and dinner, as many have now switched to having the same prices for both meals. I would recommend checking out the menus for restaurants so that you can compare prices before you go or make a reservation.

Eat a Late Lunch

When you're taking advantage of the lower lunchtime prices, I would also suggest that you eat as late as you can while still staying within the restaurant's lunch hours. I like to make a reservation for a late lunch around 2 p.m, which is still generally within the lunch menu hours. I'm usually done eating by about 3:30 p.m., which is good timing for a late lunch/early dinner.

FRUGAL DINING OPTIONS IN EACH PARK

Since I don't recommend bringing peanut butter and jelly sandwiches into the parks for meals, you'll probably have to splurge a bit by eating at the restaurants. I do enjoy eating in the parks even though the food is overpriced. It helps you feel like you're enjoying yourself more on your vacation.

What are some of the more frugal options when dining in the parks? I look at the overall value of the meals, not just the individual prices on each one.

For example, one of my favorite meals is the half rotisserie chicken at Cosmic Ray's Starlight Cafe in the Magic Kingdom. While the price is on the higher side at $10.99, you get a large amount of food for that price, which makes it a great value - half a chicken, mashed potatoes and a vegetable. If you're a big eater, you'll be quite full after eating this. If you're not, it's large enough to be split between two people or an adult and child. It's also on the healthy side, so you won't feel too guilty after finishing it!

Here are my favorite frugal dining options in each park:

MAGIC KINGDOM

I always stop at the Main Street Bakery for breakfast, which is now a Starbucks. You can get a variety of breakfast pastries for $2 - $4 or breakfast sandwiches for $5. Of course, you'll also have to get a Starbucks coffee or other drink to wash it all down, which will set you back another $2 or so.

Like I mentioned above, my best recommendation for a good value lunch is Cosmic Ray's Starlight Cafe in Tomorrowland. Not only do you get a large variety of options to choose from, but I've also found that the portion sizes are some of the largest in the park. Many of the entrees can easily be split or will fill you up for a while if you're a big eater.

Another great place to eat is the Columbia Harbor House in Liberty Square. The Columbia Harbor House is a quick-service dining option that has a heavy focus on seafood meals. You can find meals such as salads, fried fish, lobster rolls and other various seafood sandwiches. If you are dining here, be sure to check out the second floor because it's always much less crowded.

EPCOT

World Showcase at Epcot presents a large variety of dining options with many meals at very good values. One of my favorite budget dining options is the Boulangerie Patisserie in France for both breakfast and lunch. If you're arriving at the main gates, it's a bit of a hike to go just for breakfast. So I would only recommend it if you're coming in through the International Gateway entrance, which is in the back of the park.

Not only are all of the food options amazingly delicious, but they also are on the cheaper side. You can get things like quiche, croissant sandwiches and, of course, the famous pastries - all for under $5! A long line usually forms around mealtimes, but I have found that it moves quickly. So don't be deterred if you see the line. It's there for a reason.

FRUGAL TIP

THE ROSE & CROWN CHARGES OVER $20 FOR THE FISH AND CHIPS. GO RIGHT AROUND THE CORNER TO THE YORKSHIRE COUNTY FISH SHOP AND GET IT FOR ONLY $10.50.

Both Japan and China's quick-service restaurants offer an interesting variety of options, as well as good values. China's Lotus Blossom Cafe quick-service restaurant has many items such as potstickers and egg rolls for $5.25 and under. Most of the entrees are a great value for the size and come in under $10.

In Japan, the Katsura Grill features many Japanese dishes such as sushi, noodle bowls and teriyaki. My favorites are the noodle bowls, such as Udon, or the sushi, which all can be had for under $10.

Best Option for Sit-Down Restaurants at Epcot

With so many tempting culinary options available in World Showcase at Epcot, you almost have to have a dinner or lunch at one of them. The restaurants in World Showcase are by no means cheap. Unfortunately, they are actually some of the most expensive in all of Disney World.

If you do choose to splurge on a restaurant, I have a few recommendations for the best value restaurants in World Showcase.

1. **Rose and Crown Dining Room** - This is the only restaurant in World Showcase where most entrees are under $20 and most appetizers are in the $10 range. It's also worth pointing out that they have a great beer selection. If you are going to head here for dinner, I would recommend having a late dinner and sticking around to watch Illuminations from the restaurant. You'll have one of the best front row views of the show right after you're done with your dinner.

2. **Via Napoli Ristorante e Pizzeria** - This new Italian pizza restaurant in the Italy pavilion can be a great value if you order the right way. The best value meals here are the larger pizzas, which are made to be split by a few people. The smaller, individual pizzas are more than $20 a

piece and simply aren't worth the price. When you order a pizza and split it between three people, it comes to $31. This is just over $10/person - much more reasonable. The largest pizzas go for $41 and can be split between four or five people, which is an even better value.

HOLLYWOOD STUDIOS

Hollywood Studios has a few restaurant options when it comes to good and fairly inexpensive menu choices. My go-to spot is the ABC Commissary restaurant, which is a quick-service restaurant featuring a large variety of food options from salads to burgers to steak. Most entrees are in the $10-$12 range with a few salads coming in under $8.

The second place to check out for good dining options is the Sunshine Ranch Market on Sunset Blvd. The market is a collection of a few different quick-service restaurants that offer food such as turkey legs, salads, pizzas and sandwiches.

If you're looking for some breakfast options, your best bet will be the Starring Rolls Cafe on Sunset Blvd. The cafe features a variety of breakfast pastries and coffee, with all of the pastries costing between $2 and $4.

ANIMAL KINGDOM

My favorite value option at Animal Kingdom is the Flame Tree BBQ. At first glance, the prices do seem high for a quick-service restaurant, but the portions are huge so you'll be getting a lot for your money. I generally don't recommend sharing meals, but this is one place that you could order one entree, and maybe an extra side or dessert, and easily feed two hungry adults.

As I mentioned earlier in this chapter, the Yak & Yeti restaurant is in Animal Kingdom and is a great option if you are taking advantage of the Landrys gift card strategy. The quick-service Yak & Yeti also is a fairly good value because of the large portion sizes - most entrees are right around $10.

Eating a larger meal that late in the day will help to hold you off until evening, so you can make lunch your big, "main" meal. Not only will you be getting the lunch prices, but you will also have an easier time getting a reservation and the ability to stay full through dinner time.

For all of those reasons, I'm a huge fan of going to full-service, sit-down restaurants for lunch.

WHAT DO YOU MEAN A BOTTLE OF WATER IS $2.75?

Nothing pains me more than having to pay any amount of money for water, let alone more than $2.75. I'm sure you can relate to the feeling you get as you frustratingly pull out your wallet to pay for something that should probably cost much less. Disney knows they have you - It's hot and humid in central Florida, which means you'll need plenty of water during the day.

You might be thinking, "What's the big deal paying $2.75 for a bottle of water when you need it?" Well, if you do the math, it can add up very quickly. Let's say you have a family of four and are touring the parks for four days. At a minimum, you're having two meals in the parks per day: lunch and dinner.

8 meals x 4 people = 32 bottles of water total.
32 bottles x $2.75 a bottle = $88 minimum for water!

That $88 could get you an extra night in a hotel or maybe a character meal for your family. It could also just be some extra money to put back into savings. $2.75 might not seem like that much but, if you do the math, those small costs can really add up quickly.

Luckily, you have a few options when it comes to keeping the cost of water down.

Bring Water Bottles With You To The Parks

Disney has water fountains all around the parks, which are free to use. These fountains aren't generally known for their good taste. I always get a chlorine or salty taste from many of the water fountains around the park, and most of the water tends to come out lukewarm at best. However, you have to work with what you've got.

The hardest part of this tip might be that you have to carry the water bottles around with you, even when you're not using them. I never really enjoy having to lug big, clunky water bottles around. I found a nice solution to that problem: collapsible water bottles!

These water bottles fold down completely flat when not full of water, and they fold up so much that they can easily be packed away when they're not being used. If you have a family, it's much easier to carry four or five of these than it is to carry around full-sized water bottles that don't flatten out.

I like to bring along a small bag or backpack to carry a few items. This always includes empty bottles of water and some snacks for the day. You can fill up the bottles of water at any of the water fountains throughout the parks. It sure beats paying $2.75+ for a bottle!

Ask For Free Water!

I always request water from the tap, not a water bottle, when I go to a quick-service restaurant for a snack or meal. I've seen crew and staff members start to pre-fill large cups of ice water alongside cups of soda, so they are expecting guests to ask for free water. It won't be a strange request!

If you do this, be sure to ask specifically for the free "tap." A few times, I've been charged for a bottle of water when I meant the free cups. If you simply ask for water, they will give you a bottle of water. You need to specifically ask for tap water, which will cost you nothing.

Even if I'm not purchasing something from the restaurant, I've been successful in asking for a free cup of tap water without any question from the cast members. All you need to do is ask! I've even asked a few counter-service restaurants to fill up a some of my water bottles, which they did, but it might be slightly frowned upon to do that.

Bring Your Own Water In The Parks

Disney allows you to bring food and snacks into the parks, which includes bottles of water. You technically could bring in gallons of water but, realistically, you won't want to carry more than a few bottles with you. I usually freeze a few bottles the night before so that I have cold ice water for at least part of the day. When you drink the water and are still left with the frozen center of ice, you can refill your bottle at the water fountains throughout the parks.

You also don't have to limit what drinks you bring in. If you want to bring in juice or soda, that is allowed as well. Although, I would avoid bringing things in glass bottles. That would be a mess to deal with if one were to break!

I know what you might be thinking (or at least what I am) and no, unfortunately, no beer or alcoholic drinks are allowed to be brought into the parks. You can, of course, still bring your own alcohol to your resort. So just make a trip back to the room when you're in need of that cold one.

I recommend bringing a soft-sided, insulated cooler with you into the parks. The soft-sided coolers are cheaper, lighter and can easily fold down at the end of the day. This makes them easier to carry and store. Just make note that coolers can be no larger than 24" x 15" x 18" in size. If your cooler is larger, they won't let you through the front gates.

Water was a large cost for the Barry family on their last trip. They spent upwards of $30+ a day on water, which added up to a grand total of $132 over the course of their trip. After finding out how easy water is to get for free at the parks, they vowed to never actually pay money for it again.

Dad Barry took charge of this situation and already went onto Amazon to purchase four of the collapsible water bottles for their upcoming trip. They plan to use these water bottles, freeze them in their hotel rooms the night before going to the parks and ask for free cups of water at counter-service restaurants. By doing that, they should be able to get **free water for their entire trip this May!**

EATING MEALS OFF-SITE

Eating meals off-site will probably only be an option for guests that have access to a car or are staying at an off-site hotel. If you fall into either of those categories, you're going to be able to save a lot of money by eating your meals at restaurants that are not on Disney property.

Right across the street from Disney, on 535 and down International Drive, there are literally dozens and dozens of restaurant options in all types of budget ranges.

A few of my favorites are:
- Chevy's Fresh Mex
- Pizzeria Uno
- Macaroni Grill
- Bahama Breeze
- Havana's Cuban Cuisine
- Carrabba's
- + many more in the area

Compared to dining at a full-service restaurant on property, you'll probably save anywhere from 10 - 20+ percent dining at these off-site restaurants.

Remember from dining tip #1 that you can purchase discounted or free gift cards for many restaurant chains using your credit card points. Chains like Macaroni Grill, Olive Garden, Chili's, Outback Steakhouse, and many more, are available on the gift card portals. Using any of those discount gift card methods will help add to the savings of dining at an off-site restaurant.

Cardpool.com offers gift cards to just about every restaurant chain imaginable. A browse through their collection of cards shows average discounts between 10 and 21 percent, which is a nice savings. I was apprehensive to purchase from one of these gift card resellers at first, but they have two things working in their favor.
1. Cardpool offers a money back guarantee if the gift card you purchase ends up being for a different value than was stated on the site.
2. You are purchasing directly from Cardpool, not a person. The values of the gift cards are verified before they are put up for sale on the site.

I've used them to purchase various discounted gift cards with no issues to date.

Embrace Your Inner Chef
When talking about eating meals off-site, I always like to include the fact that, if you have a kitchen, you can easily cook meals in your room for even more savings. Let's not forget that we are on vacation, however, so nobody wants to cook away in the kitchen for hours after a long day in the parks. I always like to Google search quick and easy 30-minute meals that I bring along for easy dinner options.

FRUGAL TIP
ANOTHER OPTION FOR A SUPERMARKET RUN IS TO CALL AN UBER OR A CAB TO MAKE THE QUICK TRIP TO THE GROCERY STORE.

If you are staying off-site, you most likely have access to a car. This also means easy access to the many grocery stores located just off-site. Publix, Winn-Dixie and Goodings are grocery stores within a mile of Disney property that you can go to and grab some groceries for the week.

If you are staying off-site or in a Disney resort villa with a kitchen, there are local grocery delivery services available that will deliver to your resort. I know many readers that have used GardenGrocer.com. They run a special discount if you get your order in early:

- 15 days in advance = 5 percent
- 30 Days in advance = 7 percent
- 60 Days in advance = 10 percent

These discounts are taken off your subtotal. You will pay a slight premium for the delivery service, but it will save you a lot of time and effort in getting groceries to your room.

Sometimes I'll just order a pizza to be delivered to the room after a long day at the parks. You can't beat that!

Unfortunately for the Barry family, they can't travel off-site for any meals on their upcoming trip. This tip won't do them much good for now, but if they were to stay off-site and/or have access to a rental car in the future, they could take advantage of this tip for some good savings.

FREE DINING PACKAGES

One of the most popular promotions that Disney has released just about every year is the free dining package. This promotion adds the Disney Dining Package for free if you book a full-price Magic Your Way room + park ticket package.

Even though you have to book a full-price package, getting in on a free dining package can save you big bucks when it comes to your vacation. In the end, you'll still come out way ahead.

The quick-service dining plan costs $42.84 (adults) and $17.47 (children) per person per night. The full-service dining plan costs $61.84 (adults) and $20.96 (children) per person per night. If the Barry family were to pay for the dining package for their trip, it would cost them an additional $583.96 for the quick-service plan and $825.92 for the full-service dining plan.

Disney generally releases the free dining promotion during the slower times of the year to help drive visitors and keep rooms full. The biggest issue I've found with the free dining packages is there is no guarantee that a) they will release a free dining package and b) what dates the free dining promotion will be.

Looking back, here are the months that Disney has announced free dining promotions over the last few years:

- **August 2010**
- **May 2011**
- **August 2011**
- **March 2012**
- **July 2012**
- **May 2013**
- **August 2013**
- **May 2014**
- **April 2015**

Again, those were the months/years that Disney announced the free dining package. Usually, the dates of the actual promotion were for the following season. As you can see from the pattern in the dates, there are a few months during the course of the year that you could be on the watch for a free dining package announcement.

The beautiful Be Our Guest Restaurant in the Magic Kingdom

Since 2010, August and May have been the months of choice for free dining announcements. The actual travel dates for those promotions were in the fall. If we group April with May and the July dates with August, you're looking at late summer or early spring announcement dates.

There are many factors that could change when the free dining packages are announced. As mentioned, Disney uses them as marketing tools to help fill rooms during slow periods. Fall is generally a slow period, which is why we see announcements during the summer for free dining that will be applicable in the fall.

DISNEY FUN FACT
THE FAMOUS SMOKED TURKEY LEGS TAKE OVER 6 HOURS TO COOK AND OVER 1.2 MILLION POUNDS ARE SERVED EACH YEAR. GOBBLE, GOBBLE!

Booking Challenges
The biggest complaint that I hear from guests every year is the very limited number of rooms and dates that are available for the free dining packages. Disney chooses specific dates at specific resorts that are showing lower capacity to offer the package for. I have heard from people who have called up just a few days after the promotion was announced only to find that most of the dates were taken already.

Since this is such a popular promotion, many of the rooms and dates are booked immediately after the announcement is made. The very limited number of rooms are taken very quickly. If you're hoping to take advantage of a free dining package, you'll need to book as quickly as you can and be flexible with the dates you go.

Tips for Scoring a Free Dining Package
1. **Don't wait for a free dining promotion announcement to book your package.** Disney allows you to change the dates of your package, as well as apply promotions to existing bookings as they are announced. I always recommend booking on the dates you want and then keeping an eye out for a free dining announcement.

2. **Keep an eye out for an announcement on FrugalMouse.com** in the August/July or April/May timeframes. Usually, we'll start hearing about some rumors in the few weeks leading up to the official announcement. I'll post all information as soon as I hear about them.

3. **Be flexible.** If a free dining promotion is announced, be ready to book that day. You'll also need some flexibility on where you stay and when you go. Disney releases packages on specific rooms on specific days. To take advantage, you might need to adjust your vacation dates to match the promotion dates.

4. **Act quickly.** Since this is such a popular money-saving promotion, available rooms will go quickly, usually a bulk of them within a few days. Ideally, you should book the same day the promotion is announced to give you the most flexibility.

5. **Book restaurant reservations early.** Table-service restaurants will fill up very quickly after the free dining package is announced. Book your reservations at restaurants as early as you can, preferably before free dining is even announced. You can always change a reservation, so it doesn't hurt to have them in place early.

DRINKS AROUND THE WORLD

There's nothing quite like having a cold beer after a long, hard day in the parks. If you're staying at one of the Disney resorts or having a drink in the parks, you're going to pay quite the premium for that drink. Using the words "discount" and "drinks" in the same sentence is almost an oxymoron when discussing drink prices at the parks and resorts.

While Disney does offer a large variety of good drinks, they are definitely on the expensive side. Expect to pay around $6.50 for a domestic beer and $9 -11 for a premium beer, wine and cocktails. While most prices are not off the charts, paying $6 for a Bud Lite is borderline criminal.

The question is: How do you minimize the costs?

Drinks in the Parks and Resorts

I really wish I had some better news for you when it comes to ways of saving money on drinks in the parks. Unfortunately, there aren't many. Generally, I stick to beer in the parks because I find that many of the mixed drinks tend to be lacking in alcohol. If you are paying a premium for drinks at the parks, the last thing you want is to be ripped off by a weak drink regardless of how good it is.

Germany is a favorite spot to stop in for an authentic german beer!

If you want to be drinking in the parks at Disney, the reality is that you're going to have to pay for it. One exception I will mention is related to a previous strategy I shared: redeeming points for free gift cards.

Four restaurants at Disney World accept Landry's gift cards, which can also be used for drinks in the Rainforest Cafe at Downtown Disney and Animal Kingdom, the T-Rex Restaurant at Downtown Disney, and the Yak & Yeti Restaurant in Animal Kingdom.

All four of those restaurants serve drinks that can be paid for with free gift cards that you accrue through credit card sign-ups. The cocktails that all of those restaurants serve actually look very good. Plus, they serve an assortment of beers as well.

What are Our Other Options?

You'll have a few more options for cheaper alcohol after you leave the parks. My favorite go-to is to get delivery beer from Gardengrocer.com. They will deliver beer right to your resort room door, in addition to any food that you order. Just make sure you're at least 21 years old.

If you have access to a car, you will be able to purchase alcohol at any grocery or convenience store for much, much less than what Disney will charge you. As tempting as it might be to try to sneak alcohol into the parks, just don't do it. It's not worth being caught by Disney security. They'll throw it straight into the trash.

THE BARRY FAMILY'S TOTAL SAVINGS

Let's take a look back at our Barry family to see the amount of savings they will be able to take advantage of by following these easy tips.

Free Gift Cards using Points

This strategy is, perhaps, the most work out of all of the tips outlined in the book. However, it can also result in the highest savings. The Barry family was able to redeem 15,000 points and take advantage of a free $150 gift card to Landry's restaurants, which includes the Yak & Yeti, Rainforest Cafe, and T-Rex Restaurant. They decided they will use the gift card at Yak & Yeti during the fourth day of their stay. Their total savings for that dinner will be $150.

Since the meal will be free, Dad is planning to splurge on a Mahi Mahi, and Mom is already looking forward to getting a few Tropical Daiquiris (Since they'll be using this gift card near the end of their trip, Mom might need a few drinks to help her relax. Maybe you can relate!).

Total Savings: $150+

Eat Breakfast in the Hotel Room

This is one of my favorite money-saving strategies for food, and it's also one of the easiest to implement. As mentioned above, Mom Barry figured out how she can cut their total breakfast costs down from $152 to $25 by packing food to eat in their hotel room! This will allow them to save $127 on their total food bill for their trip.

Total Savings: $127+

Save Money on Water

Bottles of water, which cost around $2.75 each, are just too expensive to justify buying upwards of 20 bottles or more per trip. You can ask for free water or bring your own water bottles to negate the costs.

By using my tip of bringing their own water, as well as asking counter-service restaurants for free water, the Barry family will be able to save $132 in water costs alone!

Total Savings: $132+

Drinks Around the World

Dad Barry likes to have a cold beer after getting back from the parks each day, but the prices charged by the resorts are way too high. He's already planning to order some beer from the Green Grocer, which will help cut down on costs of beer significantly.

Total Savings: $100+

As you can see, food and drinks can really add up to a large expense during a Disney vacation. Food and drinks are necessary expenses, but they don't have to break the bank.

The Barry family's total savings on food comes out to a very generous $441! That leaves the food bill right around $300 which is much less than the $700-$1,000 that they were originally budgeting for their trip.

OTHER DISCOUNTS AND MONEY-SAVING TIPS

Now that we have covered the big ticket items - flights, hotels, park tickets and food - let's take some time to look into even more ways that you can cut down on the cost of your next Disney Vacation. Many of the money-saving strategies covered in this chapter don't quite fit into the big ticket item categories.

I want to preface this section by saying that it's difficult to predict the exact amount of savings you'll get by using the tips in this chapter. Many factors are at play. The dates you choose to take your vacation, for example, could save you $100, $1,000 or nothing at all. With that being said, they're definitely still worth looking into. You might be surprised at just how much you could save using these smaller, but still important, tips.

We're going to leave the Barry family out of this chapter for simplicity's sake, but rest assured that they will still be using many of the tips in this chapter to further reduce costs of their vacation.

What You Will Learn in this Chapter:

- The cheapest time of year to go to Disney
- What a Disney pin code is and how to get one
- What a bounceback offer is
- All about military discounts
- How the Tables in Wonderland card can save you money

WHEN IS THE CHEAPEST TIME OF YEAR TO GO?

The timing of your trip to Disney World can have a huge impact on the cost, crowds, weather and overall enjoyment of your trip. This first section focuses on the times of year when costs will probably be the lowest, and it also touches on the crowd levels during those times.

When it comes to timing your trip, the highest variable will be costs of hotels and flights because those both fluctuate greatly during the year. The second variable is crowd levels at the parks. Examining this ahead of time is important because everyone knows that **time = money**. Even though it is magical to be at Disney around Christmas, the magic quickly fades when you're constantly stuck in wall-to-wall crowds or see the hotel bill that comes with staying during the peak holiday period. I'd rather spend my time enjoying all of the attractions than waiting in all of the queues. My guess is that you and your family would too.

You'll notice that the cheapest times to go closely correspond with the off-season, which is when most people are at work and kids are in school. This is simple supply and demand. When there is a higher demand for hotel rooms and flights, the cost for those items also will be higher.

Disney tends to run additional promotions during the slower times of year to encourage people to visit. In the past, I've seen free dining plan and higher discounted room offers during certain times of the off-season.

Flights to leisure destinations like Orlando tend to decrease in price during the winter months due to lower demand. In contrast, these flights are more expensive during summer months because of increasing demand from families traveling there for their vacations.

A general tip that I always mention, especially when staying on Disney property, is that it's best to **arrive on a Sunday, Monday or Tuesday**. Disney always charges more for Friday and Saturday nights because those are the more popular nights at the resorts. By avoiding those, you'll save yourself some money on your hotel stay!

Below, I've outlined **five great times of year** to plan your trip to Disney.

1. EARLY OCTOBER

One of my favorite events takes place during this time of year - The Epcot International Food and Wine Festival. All of the countries around Epcot, including some additional ones they add for the festival, set up special stands to sell food and drinks you wouldn't normally find in the parks. Food demonstrations, celebrity chefs and special cultural shows also take place during the festival. When you pair this event with lower crowds, great weather and the **fall rate season**, you have the setup for one of my favorite times of year to visit!

One weekend to **avoid**, however, is **Columbus Day weekend.** Crowds and room rates both take a jump during that holiday weekend. Outside of that, fall is generally a less expensive and less busy season for Disney resorts and hotels.

2. LATE JANUARY/EARLY FEBRUARY

Late January and early February are also some of my favorite times to head down to Orlando. By this time, the holiday crowds are long gone; the marathon weekend is over and kids are back in school - a perfect time to visit! Just be sure to take your trip after the Martin Luther King holiday to avoid the elevated crowds and prices.

DISNEY FUN FACT

THE DISNEY MARATHON'S DOPEY CHALLENGE COMBINES A 5K, 10K, HALF-MARATHON AND FULL MARATHON RACES FOR A TOTAL OF 48.6 MILES OF RUNNING!

While much of the rest of the country can be frozen in the winter months, Orlando's climate tends to be much warmer. There could still be a few cool days here and there, however.

It also brings some of the lowest crowd levels, allowing you to hit all of the attractions with minimal wait times.

It's important to note that Disney does schedule many attraction rehabs during these less busy times, which means some may be closed. Water parks may also close down on days when it is too cold to have an enjoyable experience.

3. EARLY SEPTEMBER

A surprisingly cheap time to head to Disney World is early September after Labor Day weekend. All of the kids are back in school, leaving the crowd levels nice and light for touring. In addition, weather during September finally begins to cool down, but it will probably still be on the warmer and slightly humid side.

Early September is **value2 season** at the value resorts. This is when prices are just slightly higher than value season, but not by much.

The only potential issue to be aware of during this time of year is hurricane season. Central Florida, for the most part, is protected from the worst of the storms. However, anything that comes through could still lead to a few rainy days and possible flight delays.

4. EARLY DECEMBER

Many people think that December is a crazy time to visit Disney World because of the holiday celebrations. This is true around Christmas, and you'll probably want to be out of there by mid-December. But early December, just before the crazy rush of the holiday season, is a great time to enjoy some cheaper rates, lower park crowds and good weather.

Going in early December lets you enjoy the parks decorated for Christmas.

An added perk of being at Disney World during this time is that you'll have the opportunity to enjoy all of the amazing holiday decorations and festivities such as Mickey's Very Merry Christmas Party. Be sure to check the site for specific scheduling of the shows and festivities.

Keep an eye on dates that you'll be booking. As the season switches from fall to the holidays in mid-December, the rates and the crowd levels also switch from lower to higher.

5. EARLY NOVEMBER

Similar to early October, early November is a very good time of year to visit because of the added perk of the Epcot International Food and Wine Festival. This is also during the fall value resort season, which continues until just before Thanksgiving and helps to keep room rates down.

As you near the third week of November, crowds begin to pick up in preparation for the Thanksgiving holiday. So, for this time of year, I would stick to going within the first two weeks of November.

DISNEY PIN CODES AND HOW TO GET ONE!

One method that Disney uses to encourage people to visit is offering discount codes, which are also known as pin codes. These pin codes are coveted by many Disney fans who hope to receive them in the snail mail or their email inbox.

These pin codes can be redeemed for various discounts on rooms, tickets or packages only by the person Disney sends them to.

The question that many Disney fans have is: **How do I get targeted with a Disney pin code offer?**

WHAT ARE DISNEY PIN CODES?

Disney pin codes are exclusive offers that Disney sends out to targeted groups of people that they feel may take advantage of the offers to book discounted vacations. **Each pin code sent out is unique to that person, and it can only be redeemed by the person it was sent to.** If you were to send your pin code to someone else, **they would not be able to use it.** You must provide your last name, zip code and pin code to be able to view and redeem the offers.

Some discount codes do get released to the general public. These are codes that can be used by everyone. The pin codes I'll be talking about within this section are the ones associated with a single person - hopefully you!

You'll usually receive these pin code offers either by snail mail or email. To book a trip using a pin code, you'll need to call Disney themselves or book through a licensed Disney travel agent. When booking your vacation, tell them the alphanumeric pin code you received. This will allow them to apply the discount to your vacation.

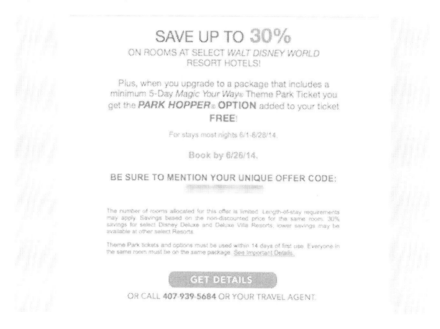

HOW DOES DISNEY USE PIN CODES?

Disney has millions of data points and analytics about us - the people that visit their parks. This is the same data that they use to send out targeted pin code offers. Disney uses pin codes in several ways to help improve their marketing:

To measure the effectiveness of their promotions. Unlike a general offer that is open to the public, they can keep track of exactly who did or did not redeem an individual pin code. This helps them analyze how effective their campaign was.

To refine their targeting. If you received a pin code offer, Disney had a reason to target you. If the reason you were targeted shows that their offers were being redeemed, they'll know it works and will use that information in the future.

To get you to visit. In the end, their main goal is to entice you with these discount offers enough that you will take action and schedule a vacation to Disney World.

HOW GOOD ARE THE DISCOUNTS?

Generally, the discounts offered by the pin codes are fairly decent. I've seen room-only discounts anywhere from 15 to 35 percent off, free dining offers and ticket upgrade offers from pin code mailings. Again, it will all vary depending on what offer Disney is sending out at the time. If things are really slow, you'll probably see better discounts to help boost room occupancy at the resorts.

HOW DO I GET A DISNEY PIN CODE?

The only way that Disney chooses people to receive pin code offers is through their targeting. The question of how to get targeted with a Disney pin code isn't an easy one to answer. How this targeting takes place is a Disney secret. **There isn't a set pattern or algorithm that has been found that will guarantee you a pin code.** What I'm sharing with you in this section is to help you improve your chances of getting an offer.

The best way **to put yourself on Disney's radar** is by giving them information that could potentially allow you to be targeted. The more Disney knows about you, the better chance you have of falling into one of their targets and receiving an pin code offer.

I receive a few Disney pin code offers a year because I have registered for just about all of the Disney online properties and have shared my information with them. While I don't know specifically what I'm being targeted by or with, **I know that registering and sharing my information with Disney has dramatically increased the frequency of pin code offers that I receive.**

Communication Preferences

☑ I'd like to receive occasional updates, special offers and other information from The Walt Disney Family of Companies.

Your first step to getting one of the coveted pin codes should be to register at the places listed below. On all of the registration forms, be sure to check the box that allows Disney to contact you with special offers - hopefully with pin codes! You may also want to set up a separate email address for all of these offers because you will be getting a lot of junk mail from Disney.

*   Sign up for a Disney account:
    https://disneyworld.disney.go.com/registration/
*   Request the free DVDs from
    https://www.disneyvacations.com/destiantions/
*   Sign up for a Disney Vacation Account (https://disneyvacationac-count.disney.go.com/), but don't actually use this.
*   Register for a Disney Cruise account:
    https://disneycruise.disney.go.com/register/
*   Go through the booking process on Disneyworld.com using your account, but don't actually book or pay.

The pin code offers will most likely come from disneydestinations@emails.disneyworld.com, so be sure to add that address to your email address book or safe list. **Don't forget to check spam filters regularly because some offers may end up there.**

BOUNCEBACK OFFERS

Disney offers special promotions to current resort guests, which are called bounceback offers. These offers are only valid when you are on your current Disney vacation. Disney offers you the opportunity to "bounce" back on another vacation before leaving your current one.

It's a smart move by Disney. You're most likely having such a great time on your current vacation that you can't wait to come back. To play to your excitement, you can take advantage of their bounceback offers.

You can find out about the current offers, if there are any, in a few ways. You may receive a flyer in your room during your stay or at check-out. You could also dial x8844 from your room and ask for an offer. The offers they provide you will usually be for a discounted room rate. To book, you'll need to pay one night's deposit before checking out.

The actual savings will vary based on the current bounceback offer. As always, be sure to do the math and check out your situation to see if this makes sense. I generally recommend against bounceback offers because they tend to be an impulse buy and don't leave a lot of time for you to plan. But, if you know for sure that you will be going back, you could be in for a good amount of savings.

DISNEY DISCOUNTS
FOR MILITARY MEMBERS

Our military allows us to have the many freedoms that we enjoy today, which includes being able to visit and have things like Disney World in our lives. Disney offers special discounts to our active and retired military personnel because of their dedication and service to our country. These discounts are on things from park tickets and hotels to special events. What a great way to honor our service men and women!

Discount Park Tickets for Military Members

Disney regularly has a park ticket special for currently active and former military members. The current promotion allows military members to get a **4-day park hopper ticket for $196 plus tax.** You can also add the Water Parks Fun & More option for an additional $34. The normal going rate for a 4-day park hopper pass is $393. This means that military members get a $197 discount on the 4-day park hopper pass - a great deal!

Note that the 4-day Water Parks Fun & More ticket will get you access into Blizzard Beach, Typhoon Lagoon, DisneyQuest, Miniature Golf and Downtown Disney. The best use of this ticket will be the water parks because of their higher admission price. Refer back to the second chapter for more details on this.

These military discount offers are time based, so you'll need to check FrugalMouse.com for current military discounts. Generally, these park ticket discounts are great to take advantage of and run for long periods of time.

To purchase the discounted 4-day park hopper passes, you will need to present your valid Military ID at the ticket booth or at the Shades of Green resort. "Eligible Service Members" are active or retired members of the U.S. military including the National Guard, Reservists and the U.S. Coast Guard.

Disney Military Hotel Discounts

Many options for hotels exist for military members, from the exclusive Shades of Green resort to the Swan and Dolphin. No matter where you stay on your Disney vacation, always be sure to ask when booking if any discounts are available to military members. Many may not be published or publicly available.

SHADES OF GREEN RESORT

The Shades of Green resort is owned and operated by the U.S. Department of Defense and is located on Disney property right across from the Polynesian resort. The resort is for active and retired military personnel and their families only. No other civilian guest can book rooms at the resort.

Compared to other Disney resorts, Shades of Green offers excellent rates, deep discounts and also has great amenities.

Shades of Green guests can take part in extra magic hours.

Guests are **not eligible** for the Magical Express airport shuttle - you'll have to rent a car or find other transportation to and from the resort.

Shades of Green resort, which is exclusive to Military members.

In order to book a room at the Shades of Green resort, you must be an active or retired member of the armed forces. See the full list of eligibility requirements: http://www.shadesofgreen.org/eligibility.htm

Below is the table of room rates for categories 1 through 3, which is based on your military grade.

SHADES OF GREEN ROOM RATES

Room Type	Category 1	Category 2	Category 3
Standard Room	$95.00	$123.00	$131.00
Poolside Room	$105.00	$133.00	$141.00
Junior Family Suite	$250.00	$250.00	$250.00
Family Suite	$275.00	$275.00	$275.00
Palm Suite	$375.00	$375.00	$375.00
Magnolia Suite	$235.00	$235.00	$235.00

Category 1: E-1 through E-5 and Cadets (E-1 through E-5 and Cadet Sponsors and dependents will receive the rate that applies to Category #1. Any additional sponsored rooms will receive the rate that applies to Category #2.)

Category 2: E-6 through E-9, O-1 through O-3, WO-1 through CW-3, Widows, Medal of Honor Recipients, 100% Disabled Veterans and Category #1 sponsored rooms (see above).

Category 3: O-4 through O-10, CW-4, CW-5, Active and Retired DoD Civilians, Foreign Military assigned to a U.S. Military installation only, DoD Contractors assigned to a U.S. Military installation only.

TABLES IN WONDERLAND CARD

An exclusive money-saving benefit to Florida Residents, Disney Vacation Club Members and annual passholders is the ability to purchase a Tables in Wonderland discount card. The card focuses on the dining experiences at the parks and resorts.

With a card, you can get **up to 10 people in your party 20 percent off dining at most restaurants** in Walt Disney World. The 20 percent discount includes alcohol and other beverages. An 18 percent gratuity is automatically added.

The card does cost **$150 for annual passholders and $175 for DVC & Florida residents**. Is it worth the cost? Let's take a look at the benefits of being a cardholder and break down some of the math to see if it is.

Tables in Wonderland Card Benefits

The biggest perk of the Tables in Wonderland card is the 20 percent discount for all food and beverage purchases at most Walt Disney World restaurants. Below is the full list of benefis:

- **20 percent discount on all food and beverage purchases (including alcohol)** at over 100 participating restaurants at the Walt Disney World Resort. Discount is valid for a party of up to 10 guests, including the member.
- **Complimentary Resort Valet and Theme Park parking** for dining purposes.
- Invitations to special events such as happy hours, dessert parties and dinners.

Is Tables in Wonderland Worth the Cost?

The Tables in Wonderland card isn't cheap. It's either $175 for Florida Residents and Disney Vacation Club Members or $150 for annual passholders.

Anytime you purchase a discount card, you want to make sure that you'll eventually come out ahead with the discounts. **What is the break even point that makes purchasing the card worth the initial fee?**

In order to see if the card would be worth the cost, you have to calculate how much you would need to spend on dining to make back the cost of the card.

- If you paid $125 for the card, **you would need to spend $875 on dining to break even.** ($875 x 20 percent discount = $175)
- If you paid $150 for the card, **you would need to spend $750 to break even.**
($750 x 20 percent discount = $150.)

That is a hefty amount of money to spend on food, but it is easily attainable for a family or if you go to the parks regularly. Before you make the purchase, do the math to see whether or not it will work in your favor.

A few words of caution about the Tables in Wonderland card:

- Replacing a lost or stolen card **will cost you a hefty $50**, so keep that card in a safe location!
- Blackout dates, where the card's perks will not be valid, are in place for the busiest days: Mother's Day, Easter Sunday, Independence Day, Thanksgiving Day, Christmas Eve, Christmas Day, New Year's Eve and New Year's Day.
- The cardholder **must be present at the meal** for the discount to be valid. You can't hand your card off to a friend or family member to get the discounts. The cardholder also **must pay for the meal** for the discount to be applied.

BOTTOM LINE

If you are able to take advantage of some of the discounts listed in this chapter, you could save yourself some big money on your next trip.

The time of year you choose to take your trip can have a large impact on cost. Disney pin codes can be hit and miss. If you really put yourself on Disney's radar, you will greatly increase your chances of getting a magical pin code in the mail. I've seen these offers range from worthless discounts to huge savings, such as free dining, so it can't hurt to get on the list.

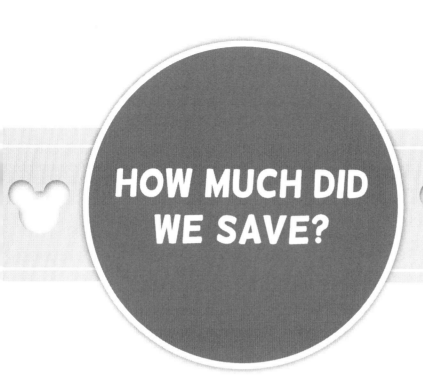

HOW MUCH DID WE SAVE?

We have reached the end of our journey together in this book, but it's just the beginning of yours. Is that affordable family vacation to Disney World starting to become easier to imagine? I sure hope so! You are now equipped with many money-saving strategies that can help you save a lot of money when you start planning your next trip.

I went through quite a bit of information within this book. If you're a little overwhelmed and aren't sure where to begin, I'd recommend picking one chapter or topic to focus on first - such as flights or hotel stays. Pick out at least one strategy and try using it on your next trip! If you're able to save $500 by using points for your hotel stay, that's already a huge victory and a big step in making your Disney vacations more affordable. Then, continue to try more strategies as you become more confident. Before you know it, you'll be the go-to person for travel savings tips amongst your family and friends.

Before we officially wrap things up, let's take one final look at the Barry family's upcoming trip to see how much money they have already saved in the planning process and still plan to save while at Disney. To recap, here is what they did to save on each of the four major areas:

- **Flights:** They opened a Southwest credit card, which awarded them a sign-up bonus of 50,000 frequent flyer miles after they paid the $99 annual fee and met the spendings requirement. They used 41,880 points + $143.80 (includes annual fee cost) to purchase their flights to Orlando.

- **Hotels:** They opened a Starwood Preferred Guest credit card, which gave them 25,000 points with no annual fee the first year. They used cash + points redemption to book a stay at the Swan for 25,000 points + $375.

- **Park Admission Tickets:** They decided not to add the park hopper option to their 4-day park passes. They purchased their admission tickets at a discount from Undercover Tourist instead, which gave them a total savings of $302.

- **Food:** They used 15,000 points to redeem a $150 Landry's gift card, which they plan to use for meals at the Yak & Yeti, Rainforest Cafe and T-Rex Cafe. They also will bring food along to eat for breakfast in hotel room and not spending any purchasing water.

Take a look at the following for the total savings of the Barry family:

Item	Original Cost	Discounted Cost	Savings
Flights	$1,000	41,880pts + $143.80	$856.20
Resort	$900	25,000pts + $375	$525
Park Tickets	$1,678	$1,376	$302
Food	$700	$259	$441
Total	**$4171.96**	**$2128.20**	**$2,124.20**

The grand total savings for the Barry family is a whopping **$2,124.20!** That's more than a 50 percent discount compared to the original cost of their trip. Taking a family of four to Disney World for just over $2,000 is quite the bargain. Let's not forget that they will be flying to Orlando and staying at one of the nicest resorts on property - the Swan and Dolphin!

There you have it! An affordable, worry-free vacation to Disney World is possible. I've done it, my friends have done it, the Barry family is going to do it - you can do it too! All of us work hard to earn a good living and raise our families. You deserve to relax and enjoy the fun things in life. I hope that, by reading and following the tips in this book, you'll be able to give your family the Disney vacation you've always dreamed of.

Did you enjoy *The Ultimate Guide to an Affordable Disney World Vacation*? If yes, I have one small favor to ask of you. I would really appreciate it if you could take a few minutes to write an honest review of the book on Amazon.com. This helps me get the word out about the book to others, which helps more people save on their Disney vacations.

Thanks again for taking the time to read the book. I am always interested in hearing reader's success stories, questions, comments and suggestions. Please feel free to reach out to me at kevin@frugalmouse.com. I would love to hear from you!

As a reminder, log onto http://www.FrugalMouse.com/bonus to claim your exclusive free bonus chapter!

Have a magical day!

RESOURCES AND LINKS

Follow Frugal Mouse for the most up to date ways to save at Disney World

http://www.FrugalMouse.com

Sign up for the Frugal Mouse Newsletter for exclusive tips and deals

http://www.frugalmouse.com/newsletter/

Like Frugal Mouse on Facebook

http://www.facebook.com/FrugalMouse/

Follow Frugal Mouse on Twitter

http://twitter.com/FrugalMouse

Frugal Mouse loves Pinning on Pinterest

http://www.pinterest.com/FrugalMouse/

Claim Your FREE Bonus Chapter at

http://www.FrugalMouse.com/Bonus

Photography by Mike Billick

Visit him at
https://facebook.com/disneyphototour/
https://www.instagram.com/disney_photo_tour/
https://twitter.com/MikeBillick
https://www.pinterest.com/DisneyPhotoTour/
http://disneyphototour.tumblr.com/
https://www.flickr.com/photos/mikebillick/

65695074R00071

Made in the USA
Lexington, KY
20 July 2017